M000307300

Community College Strategy

The Innovative Leader's Handbook

Clyne G. H. Namuo, Ph.D.

Theola,

Best of luck
to you. Enjoy!

~ Clyne

Synopsis

Community College Strategy: The Innovative Leader's Handbook is expected to be the premier guide for community college leaders everywhere and has received high praise from respected educators. Community college leaders, as well as other readers interested in our colleges, will appreciate this book because of the opportunity it provides to consider the history, current state, and future of "the people's college."

Using examples from three colleges, Dr. Clyne Namuo allows leaders to understand the importance of community colleges, their identity, and the threats they face as state funding declines. He provides specific strategies developed from his research for community college leaders, and allows us to hear from them directly toward the end of the book.

The second half of *Community College Strategy* is a handbook for leaders who strive for strategic success and innovation within the complex pressures of a community college ecosystem. In the end, Dr. Namuo recommends a new, enduring strategic position for community college leaders—a position that will develop and maintain strong, symbiotic relationships with the many stakeholders that rely on the success of our colleges.

Above all else, this book shows today's innovative community college leaders how challenging conventional wisdom can inspire us to achieve strategic success.

Praise and Endorsements
for *Community College Strategy*

"Dr. Namuo nailed it! As a former community college chief financial officer, many of the fiscal challenges outlined in this book bring back memories of challenging times—times I would like to forget. His key point about being resilient should never be overlooked. Whether community colleges learned resilience from their students or the other way around, the innovative strategies outlined in *Community College Strategy* will help guide campus leaders through the maze of decisions necessary to ensure a strong future for community colleges."

—Kevin Butler, Vice President
Finance and Business Operations, Nevada State College

"Clyne Namuo's book, like his life, expresses much of what is special about community college professionals—a combination of passionate commitment and practical pursuit of how best to serve students and communities. Namuo offers valuable insights about the challenges community college leaders face, as well as about the strategic choices they must make."

—Gary Rhoades, Ph.D.
Head, Dept. of Educational Policy Studies & Practice
Professor and Director, Center for the
Study of Higher Education
College of Education—University of Arizona

"Community college leaders will appreciate this book. It provides the opportunity to consider the history, current state, and future of "the people's college." If you are in any way concerned with the status and prospects for this country's community colleges, you owe it to yourself to read this book."

—Edward J Leach, Ph.D., CAE
Director, National Institute for
Staff and Organizational Development (NISOD)

"*Community College Strategy:* The Innovative Leader's Handbook is a must read for community college leaders of all levels. Dr. Namuo provides an in-depth look into the true meaning of the comprehensive mission of American community colleges. This book also outlines the many challenges community colleges face as they continue offering high quality services with fewer resources. Dr. Namuo's personal insights and experiences make this handbook an easy, enjoyable read. His perspectives on achieving strategic success through innovation will challenge many leaders to look differently at the work they do."

—Richard Hall, Ph.D.
Vice President of Academic Affairs
Northern Wyoming Community College District

"I've had the pleasure over the past 23 years to serve as a faculty member, department chair, dean, chief academic officer and president/CEO at a variety of community colleges. Each of these institutions, large or small, urban or rural, private or public, has faced dynamic challenges as they worked to fulfill their lofty missions of student success and community involvement in times of financial difficulties.

Dr. Namuo's book provides excellent guidance for leaders at all levels. His book allows leaders to understand the importance of community colleges, their identity, and the threats they face as state funding declines. He provides specific strategies developed from his research for community college leaders, and allows us to hear from them directly toward the end of the book. Above all else, this book provides a strategic perspective that will make you a more effective and innovative leader. Dr. Namuo's book has my highest recommendation."

—J.D. Rottweiler, Ph.D.
President, Cochise College

"As a retired community college administrator who worked in the field for almost four decades, I find Dr. Namuo's book thoughtful and compelling reading for both novice professionals and seasoned leaders. Perhaps the author's finest contribution is the readable and useful ways he presents research (his own and others); he offers useful perspectives on how leadership can drive institutional innovation and achieve strategic successes in the face of ever-increasing fiscal challenges. I highly recommend this book to all community college leaders—present and future."
—Joanna K. Michelich, Ph.D.
Executive Vice President/Provost (Ret.), Cochise College

"Clyne Namuo provides a critical perspective regarding our nation's community colleges. He adeptly argues for community colleges to take their rightful strategic place of importance in higher education. His book is a must read for anyone committed to equality, economic development, and the economic vitality of the United States of America."
—Lee D. Lambert, J.D.
Chancellor, Pima Community College

"In *Community College Strategy*, Dr. Namuo provides a useful handbook for aspiring or current community college leaders. Few researchers have attempted to study the impact of reduced financial resources on the strategic position of community colleges. Dr. Namuo accomplishes that objective while still presenting a readable, enjoyable book filled with stories and examples of leaders striving for strategic success. As a community college leader and researcher, I recommend this book to anyone involved with community colleges."
—Eric Mapp, Ph.D.
Department Chair - Business, Cochise College

"Dr. Namuo embodies the rare combination of someone who is both a scholar of community colleges and a community college administrator himself. The research and theories are strengthened by his insider perspective and tremendous respect for the value of community colleges in our society, especially given the pressures and constraints faced by the strategic leaders at the helm of these institutions that arguably represent some of the most important points of access to opportunity in our nation."

—Regina Deil-Amen, Ph.D.
Associate Professor, Center for the Study of Higher Education
Educational Policy Studies and Practice, University of Arizona

Copyright © 2014 by Clyne G.H. Namuo

NorLightsPress.com
762 State Road 458
Bedford IN 47421

All rights reserved. No part of this book may be reproduced or transmitted in any form or by any means, electronic or mechanical, including photocopying, recording or by any information storage and retrieval system, without written permission from the authors, except for the inclusion of brief quotations in a review.

Printed in the United States of America
ISBN: 978-1-935254-96-6

Cover Design by Vorris Justesen
Book Design by Nadene Carter

First printing, 2014

Dedication

This book is dedicated to my brilliant
and beautiful wife, Tiana Namuo.
You are proof that angels walk among us.

Contents

Synopsis ii

Foreword. 1

Preface 5

Chapter 1: Why Community Colleges are Important 9

   Students. 11

      Stratification and Career Paths. 14

      Student Support Services 17

      Student Life and Club Activities. 21

      Academic Rigor 24

      A Commitment to Developmental Education 27

   Economic Impact. 31

Chapter 2: The Deeply-Held Identity of Community Colleges . 35

   A Story. 36

   The Collective Identity of Community Colleges. 40

   The Evolution of the Community College Identity 41

   Federal Government Influence 41

   The Comprehensive (and expanding) Mission of
      Community Colleges. 42

   Influence of State and Local Governments 45

   Think Different (thanks, Steve Jobs) 45

Chapter 3: The Great State Divestment in Higher Education . .49

   The Great Divestment. 52

   University Response to The Great Divestment. 56

   Community College Response to Fiscal Pressures. 61

   Preview of Key Strategies 64

Literary Intermission 68

Chapter 4: The Community College Ecosystem 71

External Pressures and Identity 72

Quartering and Mandate. 73

The Quartering of Community Colleges. 73

    Community. 75

    State Government. 80

    Regulators. 81

    Other Community Colleges 83

Possessing a Mandate to Neutralize Pressures 84

The Isomophic Huddle 86

The Ecosystem. 86

Chapter 5: Community College Strategy 89

Your Ability to Lead 91

Embedded Community Colleges 93

    Embedded Activities 95

Example 1: Buffering and Neutralizing by Upper
    Administration. 96

    Effective Lobbying Activities 96

    Increased Activity of Statewide Associations 97

Example 2: Identification and Clear Communication of
    Strategic Concepts 98

Example 3: Strategic Flexibility 99

    Serendipitous Strategic Initiatives. 100

Example 4: Strategic Significance of Financial Reserves . . . 102

Example 5: Grants as Strategic Supplemental Assets 103

Example 6: Embedded Community Colleges are
    Supported Community Colleges. 105

Example 7: Active Ecosystem Awareness and Foresight . . . 106

Example 8: Shared Governance is the Spoonful of Sugar . . . 107

Example 9: Predictive Program Development 108

Conclusion 109

Chapter 6: Community College Leaders—In
    Their Own Words. 111

In Their Own Words: Strategy 113
In Their Own Words: Finances. 120

Afterword 125

Appendix—Workbooks 127
  Chapter 4: The Community College Ecosystem—
    Workbook 127
    Quartering Concept 127
    Mandate to Neutralize 128
    Discussion Questions 128
  Chapter 5: Community College Strategy—Workbook. 130
  Chapter 6: Community College Leaders—Workbook. 131

Acknowledgements 135
About the Author 137

Foreword

I joined the community college movement, and it was a movement, in 1970 when I was hired to teach introductory chemistry and political science at Leeward Community College in Hawaii. This decision wasn't a planned career move, but rather the unexpected result of a visit to a friend at the college while my wife and I visited her parents.

Once I became part of the Leeward Ohana, or family, it became clear I had joined a dedicated group of institution builders. Driven by a deep commitment to social equity and a belief that the benefits of higher education shouldn't be limited to a privileged few, these faculty and administrators—along with others around the country—set about creating the modern community college. In so doing, they created core values, or, as Dr. Namuo describes them, the normative isomorphism of community colleges: education should be affordable, access should be open, and colleges should be part of the communities they serve.

Now, more than four and a half decades later, community colleges have matured and become a vital component of our higher education landscape. Forty-five percent of all higher education students, and an even higher percentage of minority students, enroll in community colleges. The President of the United States and other political and business leaders identify community colleges as critical to developing a modern workforce in America and increasing the economic mobility of our citizens. Developing nations ranging from Indonesia, to India, to Eastern Europe and Africa, look to the U.S. community college model as they address post-secondary access in their own countries.

Along with this success has come a time for criticism and self-reflection as outlined by Dr. Namuo. Partly driven by public funding policies, the access agenda didn't always translate to students obtaining the benefits of post-secondary education. A deep commitment to helping students become prepared for post-secondary study through developmental education may have resulted in policies and practices that, in fact, formed their own barriers to student success.

Recognized as more nimble than traditional higher education, community colleges nonetheless may, in their maturity, have become less able to react to economic changes. As higher education financing becomes a national and state public policy issue, even the affordable community colleges are challenged to examine not only the cost of attendance, but also the costs of graduation or transfer success, and to find ways to drive down those costs.

In *Community College Strategy*, Dr. Namuo provides a guide for navigating the new community college world. This is not a GPS type of guide – "turn right in 200 yards for improved student success." Rather, it weaves stories and experiences of students and practitioners into the broader social and political environment in which colleges find themselves. This grounding in reality, combined with external forces, provides a valuable framework for anyone who is committed to the continuing development and improvement of community colleges.

I'm particularly intrigued by the vision of embedded community colleges and their rigorous, mature commitment to local communities as part of our original values. Becoming embedded allows colleges to not only react and respond to workforce and social needs in a community, but also lets us contribute to local economies and their social infrastructures. Becoming embedded allows colleges to tap into a much richer array of services, industry connections, and less traditional educational opportunities beyond what the college can do by itself. Becoming an integral part of a community benefits both students and their colleges as we navigate the external forces identified by Dr. Namuo.

I'm not sure where the next decades will take community colleges. I suspect much of the change will be about boundary blurring. Students will not graduate from high school and go to college. They will continue their education at a community college, having begun their post-secondary education while still in high school. Similarly, community college students will not complete their AA degree and transfer to a baccalaureate school. They will begin working toward a baccalaureate from day one at the community college, on a pathway that is clearly marked, available, and reliable. Community college students will not go to school and then go to work. Work and education will blend over the working lifetime of the student—sometimes in a classroom or laboratory, sometimes on-line, and sometimes on the job.

I also suspect we will become much more sophisticated in our use of technology. Can you imagine using a Walmart style supply-chain in a community college environment? What if we had the ability to identify and deliver just-in-time work force training, just-in-time development education, and just-in-time support services through a system that could tap into resources from sister colleges? Where will technology take us in terms of flipped classrooms, open education resources, simulations, and a more refined understanding of our students and their barriers?

Community College Strategy offers a valuable framework for both emerging leaders and the seasoned leader who has become immersed in day to day work and needs a framework for

addressing the issues in our changing environment. Although each community college is different, Dr. Namuo points out that we have much in common: a commitment to social equity through affordable, successful, community-based higher education. That is what makes us unique and what makes us successful. —John Morton, Ph.D.
Vice-President for Community Colleges
University of Hawaii

Preface

One of my favorite recurring conversations with my two oldest sons (ages seven and nine years) involves their future professions. "So, what do you want to be when you grow up?" I ask. Their aspirations have evolved over the years, starting with:

"Fireman."

"Policeman."

"Superman."

"Batman."

These were the prime choices when they were younger. Their answers are now a bit more sophisticated. My middle son most recently responded with "Astrophysicist." Whoa. Well, the Stephen Hawking special we watched together might explain his response. My oldest responded with "Veterinarian," and considering his love for animals that makes perfect sense. Over the years, my advice to them hasn't changed: "Do something you're passionate about." I give that same advice to the students who enroll in my college classes.

I was fortunate to turn a hobby and passion into a career. Because of this, I've been able to touch thousands of lives over the years and still look forward to my job every day. I am the Department Chair for Computer Information Systems at Cochise College in southeastern Arizona. In addition to teaching courses, my administrative responsibilities allow me to become involved in a variety of projects affecting my department, my field, and the entire college.

I have lived in three cities: Honolulu, San Diego, and Sierra Vista, Arizona. Yes, one of these cities is NOT like the others. However, this is where I discovered my second passion: community colleges. I recently completed a Ph.D. in Higher Education Strategy from the University of Arizona's Center for the Study of Higher Education. My dissertation is titled "Reduced Financial Resources and the Strategic Positioning of Community Colleges: How an Embedded Community College Can Neutralize External Pressures."

This tongue-twisting title was written for academia; not intended for mass consumption by people who don't wear elbow pads on their sports coats. However, as I visited conferences to present the results of my research to academics and practitioners, I realized my message—the plain-English version—is something community college leaders deeply care about. The question driving my research was something they ALL dealt with.

> *Community College Strategy* offers a concise, plain-English examination of what makes a community college strategically successful.

Everywhere in the United States, community colleges struggle with decreased allocations from government sources. This leads to dire consequences for schools that are not used to managing such drastic cuts. Arizona reduced its allocation to community colleges by almost fifty percent. Devastating. California sliced the allocation to its community college system by eight percent, which may not seem huge until you consider that eight percent is actually five hundred twenty million dollars, and affects approximately three million students in their system. Devastating. Around the same time, the state of Illinois reduced appropriations to community colleges by approximately fifty percent. Devastating.

Devastating because the Great Recession is upon us, and history and research show that community college enrollments soar during tough economic times.

Devastating because at a time when many community colleges are seeing record enrollments they must handle droves of new students, yet these schools have fewer resources than ever before.

That's how it is with the new economy. As one community college president shared with me "Community colleges have been their own worst enemies because whenever the state cuts, we find a way. We just find a way to get it done."

"Getting it done" is the theme of my book. *Community College Strategy* highlights the amazing resilience of community college leaders who find innovative ways to handle financial reductions. My conclusions are built on a foundation of higher education research at the highest level, accumulated during my year-long dissertation research as I visited twenty-seven community college leaders across three separate colleges.

Within these pages you'll find real-life stories and real-world examples of research in action. This is my attempt to connect the two worlds I straddle: researcher and practitioner.

If you're looking for an overly technical, academic text, then this isn't the book for you. *Community College Strategy* offers a concise, plain-English examination of what makes a community college strategically successful. These stories will inspire you to become a more effective leader—and give you the tools and perspective to create truly innovative strategies that will move your college in exciting and sustainable strategic directions.

Also, please direct your attention to the appendix at the end of this book as I have created workbooks to supplement the second half of this book. Chapters 4, 5, & 6 contain specific strategies to facilitate strategic success. These workbooks will help you convert these concepts into practical strategies.

Chapter 1

Why Community Colleges are Important

*M*any people believe community colleges serve only as a last resort for people who can't get into four-year schools. As author Isa Adney described it, "On my first day of community college, I cried like a little girl. Like so many students I've met since then, I didn't want to be there. I felt alone, dejected and lost."

But Adney quickly changed her mind. Six years later, having graduated with honors and obtained a master's degree, she wrote the book *Community College Success* and works with Pearson Education to promote community colleges. Now, she says, "Community college is a smart choice. These schools don't let just anyone in . . . they accept *everyone* who wants an education. That's something to be proud of. After a year in community college I began telling people it was like a private-school experience at public-school cost."

I hope to show you why community colleges should no longer be considered the lowest common denominator in higher education and that the denigration of these schools needs to stop.

Community colleges exist to positively transform lives—and that's exactly what they do.

The stigma attached to community colleges no longer applies, and they should not be treated (as one administrator aptly put it) "like the last pig at the trough." These dynamic, innovative schools have proven their resilience time and time again.

Thus, *Community College Strategy* goes beyond giving strategic tools to community college leaders. I want to help community colleges take their rightful strategic place in higher education. When you finish this book, you will understand the true power of the community college system and its ability to have long-lasting, wide-ranging effects on the communities that rely on our graduates, our economic might, and our strategic prowess.

> *Community College Strategy* goes beyond giving strategic tools to community college leaders. I want to help community colleges take their rightful strategic place in higher education.

This chapter will focus on two perspectives to explore the basic impact of community colleges. First, I examine three factors behind the influence of these schools: their impact on students' social mobility; their focus on teaching and learning (as opposed to the research-focused agenda of most universities), and their commitment to the philosophy of open access and everything that entails.

We will look at the challenges most often encountered by community college students and consider how we, as leaders, can help them overcome those obstacles. Much of what I present in this first section comes from my interactions with students over the years, but my findings are supported by higher education research conducted by some of the most respected scholars in the field.

Second, I examine the economic impact of community colleges and the strategic importance of that impact for the future. While many urban community colleges claim large enrollments and budgets to match, they can also be subordinated to the whims of private industry and the demands of four-year universities. On the other hand, many rural community colleges enjoy a more elevated status as the dominant provider of higher education in their respective geographic areas. The bonds formed by rural community colleges and their communities are unique and treated as such in this book.

In this section I call upon the current activities of a handful of community colleges, my research on "Embedded Community Colleges," and selected economic data. This chapter (actually all chapters) attempt to combine the experiences of practicing community college leaders with the findings and contributions of respected higher education researchers to arrive at thoughtful and useful tools for today's innovative leaders.

Students

I began teaching part-time at a community college in my early twenties, which may seem a bit young until you consider the demand for instructors with technology expertise during the late 90s and early 2000s. This was a time when anything dot com was going public for billions of dollars and anything with the word *tech* attached to it was assigned a mythical, revered, and often undeserved status. After all, this was a time of irrational exuberance, as Alan Greenspan explained. This was also a time for the unprecedented expansion of the internet's fiber optic infrastructure to rural areas of the U.S. and the exponential increase of bandwidth between continents as well.

Being proficient with technology afforded me a wide variety of professional experiences in a number of different capacities: as a consultant, an employee, and an educator. Technology expertise remains one of my most valuable assets, and the ability to communicate technical concepts to a non-technical audience proved an essential skill as a college professor.

In 1999, I graduated with a bachelor's degree from the University of Hawaii, then immediately took a job as the information technology manager for a local tour-boat operator (think Gilligan's Island and three-hour tours). I was in over my head and loved every minute of it. I devoured new information and lived to understand the new technologies around me. This seemingly magical world of technology began to make more and more sense. I felt as though I could see the world and its future at the same time. During these exciting months I came into contact with a woman who ran a technology education center at a community college in Hawaii. I'd never taught a class before, but like all other technology-related challenges, I dove in.

I never looked back. I've been teaching technology courses at the community college level for almost 15 years and have loved every minute of it and enjoy the start of each semester. I still look forward to giving the lectures I have now memorized. I still enjoy teaching my students to become cyber criminals (perhaps I will explain that in another book). I savor each graduation as if it were my own. I delight in challenging my students to extend their learning beyond the classroom while participating in technology community service projects.

I love the community college environment. I'm sure many other teachers feel the same way. As an adjunct faculty member with the University of Hawaii Community College system and the San Diego Community College district, I taught a number of evening courses in different areas of technology (all the while working full-time in the technology industry in various positions). The more I learned about my students and their stories, the more I loved teaching those classes. I met single moms going to school at night to give themselves better opportunities. I saw working professionals wanting to advance in their jobs. Many students attended because community college tuition was cheaper than university tuition. There were students with bachelor's degrees looking to increase their technology skills.

All of these were students I could root for. They had lives and responsibilities, but they chose to sit in my class twice a week for three hours. While my class wasn't the center of their universe, their work ethic seemed to exceed that of the students I met as a university undergrad. Some struggled with English as their second language. Most were actively engaged in class and pushed me to share concepts beyond the scope of the class, but well within my area of expertise as an IT Manager or systems administrator.

I have now been a full-time faculty member at Cochise College, a community college in southeastern Arizona, for nine years—and I still find that our students are easy to root for. Many of the students at Cochise College are first-generation students who struggle with issues in and out of the classroom. Many of them come early to class and stay long after class is finished. Many of my current students juggle the responsibilities of being a parent, an employee, and a student. There are many wonderful things to love about the community college environment, and our students are certainly one of them.

> The challenge for community college leaders who want to contribute beyond their teaching duties is to maintain a meaningful connection with students.

The challenge for many community college leaders is that the higher you climb up the hierarchy in your institution, the further you move from students. As a faculty member you're at the center of the institution and its mission: teaching and learning. As a department chair you combine teaching responsibilities with administrative responsibilities that take you a little further from students. As a dean, you're further still. As a vice president or president, while your decisions might affect the entire institution, you're as far away from student contact as you've ever been.

Therefore, the challenge for community college leaders who want to contribute beyond their teaching duties is to maintain a meaningful connection with students. The most effective way to do this is to teach a class at least once a year. Despite the demands on your time and the apparent absence of available time slots in your schedule, teaching a class will reconnect you with our student population. One of the vice presidents I interviewed as part of my research made numerous references to his move to the "dark side" (from faculty to administration). When pressed about those comments, he told me how much he missed the connection with students. He missed the satisfaction that came from being in a classroom. He missed teaching.

We have to start by admitting that inequality exists in higher education and is perpetuated by institutional policies and social constructs.

If you choose to teach a class while serving as an administrator, not only will you be able to relate to our most important group of stakeholders (our students)—you will also enhance your insight into faculty concerns. When faculty members discuss their latest issues regarding the college's migration to a new learning management system, you will have first-hand experience with it. When they come to you about issues with entering final grades or other reporting requirements, your response will be more than academic. Also, you may rediscover why you got into this line of work in the first place, and perhaps you'll find yourself illuminating the infamous "dark side."

Stratification and Career Paths

"I was scared I wasn't going to go anywhere after attending a community college, but that idea changed when I met so many influential people who went to community colleges."
– Sana, Seminole State College of Florida.

We have to start by admitting that inequality exists in higher education and is perpetuated by institutional policies and social constructs. Human beings have a need to categorize and stratify things, based on criteria that don't always make sense. In higher education we find institutional stratification (Ivy League versus community colleges), social stratification (rich versus poor), and stratification based on access to higher education and success. Scholars agree that stratification exists, but they hotly debate the root causes and how best to neutralize its negative effects. Study after study demonstrates the struggles of minorities and the poor in higher education. A study conducted by Alexander Astin and Leticia Oseguera and published in *The Review of Higher Education*[1] in 2004, showed that students from wealthy families were two times more likely to attend highly selective universities than students from poor families. Additionally, they found the inequalities that existed thirty years ago have actually *increased* during the past twenty-five years.

On a more positive note, many studies demonstrate more than just isolated pockets of success for our students. For example, in an article published in 1996 in *The Journal of Higher Education*[2], Yangjing Lin and Paul Vogt demonstrated that among a sample of 30,000 community college students, associate's degree completers earned more on average than students who continued on to a university and completed bachelor's degrees. This was a controversial finding at the time.

How is it possible that people with associate's degrees were earning more than their counterparts who had bachelor's degrees? Allow me to offer some possible explanations using my institution as an example: First, let's look at the field of nursing. In the state of Arizona, approximately 75 percent of registered nurses hold no higher than an associate's degree because that's all they need to take the RN exam. Consequently, we have approximately 100 students each year at Cochise College who graduate with an associate's degree in nursing, take and pass the RN exam, then start making an average of $30.80 an hour in

---

1 Astin, Alexander W., and Leticia Oseguera. "The declining" equity" of American higher education." *The Review of Higher Education* 27, no. 3 (2004): 321-341.

2 Lin, Yangjing, and W. Paul Vogt. "Occupational outcomes for students earning two-year college degrees: Income, status, and equity." *The Journal of Higher Education* (1996): 446-475.

Cochise County (according to Economic Modeling Specialists http://www.economicmodeling.com) for an annual salary of $64,064. This is just slightly under the national average of $31.48 an hour with an annual salary of $65,478

Second, consider the impact in my area of expertise: technology. As in many parts of the country, employment in Arizona is heavily influenced by large federal and state government entities. Fort Huachuca is home to many of the Army's important commands, such as the U.S. Army Intelligence Center and the U.S. Army Network Enterprise Technology Command (NETCOM). The latter entity drives much of what we do in the Computer Information Systems department at Cochise College because many of our graduates end up working directly for NETCOM or for one of their many supporting contractors such as General Dynamics, TASC, STG, or SAIC to name a few. In 2005, the Chief Information Officer and Assistant Secretary for the Department of Defense, John G. Grimes issued a directive across all branches of the military and their supporting agencies. This directive (8570.01-M) required all individuals working in any technology-related field to pass one or multiple (depending on their jobs) industry-recognized certification exams or face termination. This directive remains in place today and led to a scenario whereby industry certification is actually more valuable than a college degree.

In response to this directive, we modified some of our curriculum to align with the objectives of the industry certification exams. As a result, many of our students graduate with not only an associate's degree but also the necessary industry certification as required by the Department of Defense directive 8570.01-M. Network and Systems Administrators in Cochise County earn $34.18 an hour for an annual salary of $71,094. While we encourage our students to continue on to a university, many choose to enter the workforce after earning their associate's degree. They find it difficult to turn their backs on such a lucrative opportunity.

Some students return later to pursue a bachelor's degree when they realize that, while industry certifications allowed them to enter the job market, a bachelor's degree allows them to stay there and to advance in their careers.

> The myth that earning an associate's degree at a community college is not worthwhile is just that: a myth.

Consider another example on the other side of the career path equation: Elementary school teachers are required to earn a bachelor's degree and, in many states, must complete an additional state-level teaching certification. In Cochise County, elementary school teachers earn $18.22 an hour for an annual salary of $37,898. This is obviously much less than the salaries of nurses and technology graduates.

In short, a student's choice of major could have an enormous impact on their earning power and the myth that earning an associate's degree at a community college is not worthwhile is just that: a myth. While community colleges may never credential doctors or lawyers, that doesn't mean lucrative career paths are the exclusive domain of four-year universities. In fact, as I have shown, the direct-employment credentials offered by community colleges can result in well-paying jobs and gainful career paths.

Student Support Services

"... I was a first-generation college student from a background of limited financial means who never graduated from high school. In approximately one year I went from being homeless to being enrolled in college, but I didn't have the support of parents, high school counselors, or even friends to guide me through the process. I felt completely lost. My wonderful community college provided resources to assist me with my entire journey."

—Steve, Valencia College and Emory University

Anyone who's worked at a community college or spent time with our students can confirm what researchers have asserted for years: Our students are more likely to come from lower socioeconomic backgrounds than their university counterparts. Our students are more likely to need some form of remedial or developmental education. Our students are more likely to be first-generation students, thereby lacking the important guidance many of their university counterparts enjoy. Our students have typically faced more obstacles than their university counterparts, and while many of our students aspire to transfer to a university, they often struggle to integrate and assimilate into university life once they get there. To compound this issue, many universities lack effective programs to assist transfer students from community colleges.

In the real world, these students face daunting challenges as they navigate the higher education landscape. Fortunately, research findings have helped schools across the country develop programs to help neutralize the negative effects students face from social and institutional barriers.

The support you provide could mean the difference between success and failure; persistence and dropping out.

Many of you reading this book are involved in such programs, and your efforts have a positive impact for your institution. The support you provide could mean the difference between success and failure; persistence and dropping out. The more you understand your unique student population, the better you'll become at building support programs to help them succeed.

These support systems are an intrinsic part of community colleges across the country, and we demonstrate this by investing in these programs and the dedicated staff to support them.

According to Mark Boggie, Assistant Dean of Student Services at Cochise College, effective student support programs have three components:

1. **Logistics:** Successful support programs help students find their way around campus, familiarize them with facilities, and help them navigate the bureaucracy of higher education. New student orientation helps with this.

2. **Expectations:** Support programs help students understand what's expected of them. This refers to academic expectations, but may also include financial aid deadlines, acquiring textbooks, study habits, and time management. Many support programs cover these topics by offering one-credit courses that meet for an hour a week.

3. **Relationships:** Successful support programs help students establish meaningful relationships with other students, faculty members, student mentors, and staff to help guide them through new experiences in higher education.

Community colleges have aggressively sought federal, state, and private funding to support programs such as the federally-funded TRIO student support services program (http://www2. ed.gov/programs/triostudsupp). In fiscal year 2013, the federal government awarded over $274 million in TRIO support services grants to over a thousand institutions. The TRIO program at Cochise College supports 160 low-income (based on federal guidelines) students or first-generation students through advising, counseling, and other assistance during the academic year. This $235,000 program (annually) is maintained by a dedicated staff of just four people who work diligently to ensure all 160 students are on track to successfully complete an associate's degree.

Unfortunately, these programs are among the first to fall during lean budget cycles when administrators look for ways to trim everything beyond instruction. A 2012 article in *USA Today*[3] says that. . .

---

3 Marklein, Mary Beth. "Community Colleges Downsize Programs." USA Today. March 19, 2012,

"Community colleges across the USA, faced with tight budgets and competing priorities, are downsizing or shuttering programs that in many cases have been held near and dear for years by students and other local constituents."

These cuts include sports programs, free community classes, and—most troubling—remedial classes for incoming students who need help with reading, writing, math, and study skills. Students can survive without sports and communities will be fine without the free classes on bread-making and financial planning; but how many non-traditional students will fall by the wayside without support services that help them break through barriers?

If we truly want students to succeed, student support programs should be close to the heart of our community colleges.

I encourage student support services leaders to participate in a constant and convincing dialogue with the leaders of your institution regarding the essential nature of your programs and the impact those services have on the stated goals of your institution. For example, TRIO programs are required to report persistence and completion data to the federal government. Considering the current national emphasis on credential completion, this would seem to place the TRIO program close to the core of any school, essential to meeting the goal of increasing the number of students who complete the program and graduate.

Many student support services leaders will fight this proximity-to-the-core legitimacy battle their entire careers.

Many student support services leaders will fight this proximity-to-the-core legitimacy battle their entire careers. Instruction has, and always will be what Burton Clark[4] refers to as the "steering core" of each college. However, we now have

4 Clark, Burton R. Creating Entrepreneurial Universities: Organizational Pathways of Transformation. Issues in Higher Education. Elsevier Science Regional Sales, 665 Avenue of the Americas, New York, NY 10010 (paperback: ISBN-0-08-0433545; hardcover: ISBN-0-08-0433421)., 1998.

research and evidence to support the argument that support services are an essential complement to instruction (think pencils and erasers).

> Student services will never replace instruction as the core function of the institution, but the more these two services can be packaged or bundled, the stronger student services will be.

How best to accomplish this goal? The answer is integration. Student services will never replace instruction as the core function of the institution, but the more these two services can be packaged or bundled, the stronger student services will be. The strategic position of student support services within the institution will be fortified, and the more it's fortified, the less likely it is to get cut during tough budgetary times. Let's look at specific scenarios related to student services.

Student Life and Club Activities

> "Joining clubs changes the way you see your college. I loved going to school every day knowing I was going to a club meeting."
> —Ashley, Pasco-Hernando Community College

Student life and club activities serve two vital purposes at a community college. First, these activities help integrate new students into college life. This eases the social and academic transition from high school by providing peer and staff supports. Vincent Tinto is perhaps the most recognized scholar in the area of student persistence through college. His seminal work published in 1975 referred to as "Tinto's Student Integration Model[5]" contends that students' connection to their institution is as important as their academic efforts. Tinto's work demonstrated the importance of integrating academic

---

5 Tinto, Vincent. "Dropout from higher education: A theoretical synthesis of recent research." *Review of educational research* (1975): 89-125.

and social activities to improve a student's college experience and to ultimately increase their chances of success. So, the next time you stumble upon a "welcome back to school" barbeque, consider being involved the next time around as an organizer, or find a way to help promote the event.

Students who involve themselves in club activities or other student life-related activities are more likely to be successful, complete all their classes, and transfer to a university.

We have a large, grassy field in the middle of the Sierra Vista campus at Cochise College. On any given day you can find our students lying out in the Arizona sun with friends, throwing a football back and forth, playing Frisbee, or other activities. The academic in me questions whether they've completed all their homework and are current with their studies. The community college leader in me usually puts the academic me in place. Often I end up taking a photo of our version of "the quad" and posting it on Twitter for all to see. I know that students who involve themselves in club activities or other student life-related activities are more likely to be successful, complete all their classes, and transfer to a university. As leaders, the degree to which we support these programs has a direct impact on the success of our students. Sometimes the academic in me still wrestles with the value of lawn bowling, but student life not only enlivens our campuses—it also strengthens the connection between students and their schools. As an innovative leader, supporting these activities may go against the stodgy traditions of your institution. Don't fear being different. Don't be afraid to make distinctive choices that oppose traditions. Innovative leaders challenge the status quo. They push institutions forward through ideas that may not be comfortable. Innovative leaders change things. You are that type of leader.

Student life and club activities also serve as a bridge between instruction and free time activities. This not only helps the students, it also strengthens the strategic position of student support services within your community college. Earlier, I mentioned the importance of packaging support services with instruction. This is one way to do that.

Most clubs are led by a faculty advisor, and these advisors are usually the most motivated and involved faculty members. Motivated and effective faculty members are those who not only develop new and exciting ways to communicate their expertise to students, but they also challenge students to extend learning beyond the classroom.

They are faculty members like Ken Charters, a biology instructor at Cochise College who can be seen leading his classes on field trips around campus to explore Arizona's unique desert plant life.

They are faculty members like Dan Guilmette, a computer information systems instructor at Cochise College who, as faculty advisor for the AFCEA club (Armed Forces Communications and Electronics Association), coordinates an annual event called Computer Challenge, a day-long competition for middle school and high school students that awards medals (gold, silver, and bronze) for events like extemporaneous speaking, information security theory, and computer repair.

They are faculty members like Dr. Jenny Krestow, an Assistant Professor and Department Chair of Astronomy at Glendale Community College who uses *scientific method of inquiry* and *project-based learning* along with cutting-edge technology like the sky-skan digital planetarium to give her students an immersive learning experience.

They are faculty members like Dr. Melissa Barlett at Mohawk Valley Community College who uses a "flipped classroom" approach that requires students to prepare heavily before class, resulting in more productive class sessions.

If you are a student support services leader, I encourage you to recruit the most innovative and inspirational members of the faculty at your institution. Remember, as an innovative leader, you are changing things. You are leaving stodgy traditions behind, and one of those outmoded traditions is the 38th parallel between instruction and student services. By recruiting these faculty leaders to be involved as faculty club advisors or in other student life activities, you will be strengthening the strategic position of student services at your institution.

When faculty members are on your team, you'll find it easier to convince others that support services and instruction should go hand in hand.

Academic Rigor

In their 2005 article "Triumph of the Education Gospel,[6]" W. Norton Grubb and Martin Lazerson point out that society now places a high value on education—a value that has become gospel. This gospel of education is founded on mastery needed for new occupations based on technology, with emphasis on the twenty-first century skills of communication, problem solving, and reasoning.

> Society now places a high value on education—a value that has become gospel. This gospel of education is founded on mastery needed for new occupations based on technology.

These authors show that higher education provides an essential service in all fields, and the public agrees with this. The education gospel has created a huge influx of students into higher education. The need to upgrade job-related skills especially affects community colleges, where technical courses are most likely to be offered.

What does this mean for community college leaders? It means our students do understand the value of higher education. They aspire to be college graduates. They know that going to college

---

6   Grubb, W. Norton, and Marvin Lazerson. "Vocationalism in higher education: The triumph of the education gospel." *The Journal of Higher Education* 76, no. 1 (2005): 1-25

is a noble, profitable, long-term life strategy. They understand that higher education is the path to a financially stable and professionally fulfilling future. College is gospel.

However, one significant downside to these widespread aspirations is that student expectations tend to be unrealistic. They want a college degree, but they may not be entirely prepared for college-level work. They know they want to graduate from college, but they may not know how to get there and what to do once they arrive.

> One could easily argue that community colleges are a safe place for students to land if they fail to meet their lofty academic goals.

In 2006, a group of researchers from Florida State University published an article in the journal *Social Problems*[7] that asked the provocative question "Have Adolescents Become Too Ambitious?" When the researchers compared high school seniors' career plans with the typical achievements of young adults, they confirmed that ambitions far outpace what these students can hope to achieve. Furthermore, aiming too high and failing creates an increased risk of depression.

One could easily argue that community colleges are a safe place for students to land if they fail to meet their lofty academic goals. Certainly, the renowned scholar Burton Clark[8] felt this way. He recognized and labeled this phenomenon as "cooling out." He argued that community colleges should help students recalibrate their expectations and direct students to more realistic academic paths. For example, a student entering community college with hopes of transferring to a university to become an engineer may find the curriculum too difficult.

---

[7] Reynolds, John, Michael Stewart, Ryan MacDonald, and Lacey Sischo. "Have adolescents become too ambitious? High school seniors' educational and occupational plans, 1976 to 2000." (2006): 186-206.

[8] Clark, Burton R., "The "cooling-out" function in higher education." *American Journal of Sociology* (1960): 569-576.

Instead of allowing the student to drop out of the community college, faculty and staff can subtly guide them into a technician-level path where credential completion is more likely.

I see this every semester at Cochise College. Some of our computer science majors aspire to be software developers, but at some point they realize that Calculus 3 is beyond reach and Differential Equations may just as well be a foreign language. At this point, we recommend they use their existing credits toward a different information systems degree, perhaps an Associate's of Applied Science degree in cyber security, or networking. As community college leaders, it's important to provide our students with options.

Many students who attend a community college are surprised

> Many students who attend a community college are surprised by the rigor of their courses.

by the rigor of their courses. They assume a community college is easier than a university. They face a harsh reality if they cling to that false assumption beyond their first semester.

Community colleges tend to have two types of courses: Those designed to transfer to a university, and courses designed to prepare students for employment (direct-employment programs). Most institutions focus more on one or the other, but all community colleges offer both types of courses.

For transfer courses, a negotiation must exist between faculty at the community college and faculty of a university. Instructors at both institutions must agree on the content of each course and its objectives. Ideally, a university-level course offered at a community college, such as ENG101, will mirror an equal class at the university. That explains why transfer courses at a community college are just as difficult as those offered at a university. However, students at a community college have the advantages of lower tuition, smaller class sizes, and more time with their instructors.

Community college faculty members have the advantage of focusing on one objective: teaching. University faculty have "publish or perish" demands and usually teach three courses per semester, while community college faculty focus solely on teaching and learning, without research requirements. Consequently, students get all of their attention.

A Commitment to Developmental Education

In Chapter Two, I will analyze the deeply-held identity of community colleges and how we, as institutions, have managed to solidify our role as open-access institutions, deeply committed to serving our traditionally disadvantaged student population. We have managed to maintain our commitments, even as we make strategic changes based on unprecedented financial reductions.

> Community college faculty members have the advantage of focusing on one objective: teaching.

Among other things, we now devote immense resources to satisfying the ever-changing compliance requirements of federal financial aid. Doing so demonstrates our commitment to the large percentage of our students who come from low socio-economic backgrounds.

I'd like you to also think about our commitment to developmental education, its impact on our students, and what it means for the strategic position of community colleges. In a speech at the League for the Innovation in Community College Conference in March of 2014, I argued that community colleges no longer occupy a fixed strategic position in higher education. We have been spreading our strategic wings for some time now. We are no longer simply seated and settled, fixed and nestled into a restrictive strategic position between our K-12 and university partners.

We are dynamic institutions challenging our traditional boundaries. We perform adult basic education functions through our GED programs. We are heavily committed to an open-access mission, and that commitment is reinforced by our developmental or remedial programs for students who aren't yet ready for college-level work. Through many different types of articulation agreements, students are now able to take three or even four years of credits toward their bachelor's degrees.

> We are dynamic institutions challenging our traditional boundaries.

And yes, some community colleges have started to offer four-year credentials. Let's take a closer look at our commitment to developmental or remedial education.

In Arizona, as in many other states, public four-year universities are prohibited from offering remedial courses. I suppose the rationale is that states don't want to pay for the same type of education twice. They believe students should have been prepared for college in high school. The reality is that many students who want to enter college do need remedial help with reading, writing, or math.

In 2011, Regina Deil-Amen (my dissertation chair) authored a chapter in a publication titled *Marginalized Students: New Directions for Community Colleges*. Her chapter is called "Beyond Remedial Dichotomies: Are Underprepared College Students a Marginalized Majority?".[9] She cites studies that show between 60-75 percent of community college students need some form of remediation before they can handle college-level work. Evidently these students are not getting the level of instruction they need from the K-12 system. However, we are not going to give up on them, and community colleges have come to the remedial rescue.

---

9   Deil-Amen, Regina. "Beyond remedial dichotomies: Are 'underprepared' college students a marginalized majority?." *New Directions for Community Colleges* 2011, no. 155 (2011): 59-71.

Dr. Deil-Amen cites the University of Arizona's remedial education relationship with Pima Community College, just down the street. Approximately 33 percent of the University of Arizona's incoming freshman class places into remedial or developmental math (any math class below the lowest level offered by the University of Arizona). These students are expected to take their remedial classes at Pima Community College as concurrent enrollees to the university or before entering the university.

Sixty to seventy-five percent of community college students need some form of remediation before they can handle college-level work.

Community colleges have embraced their role as providers of remedial or developmental education. Strategically, we could have responded differently, but that would not have supported our mission as open-access institutions. National organizations like Complete College America and The Lumina Foundation (through its Achieving the Dream initiative) have devoted considerable resources to studying the issue of remedial education and proposing frameworks and tools to better improve its delivery at community colleges. We have mobilized and organized through professional associations such as the National Association for Developmental Education (http://www.nade.net), The Council of Learning Assistance and Developmental Education Associations (http://www.cladea. net), and The National Center for Developmental Education at Appalachian State University (http://ncde.appstate.edu). We have also organized annual conferences to share best practices and research. Community colleges have faced the challenge (some might say, *burden*) as providers of remedial education with enthusiasm and determination because we believe in our open-access mission. We believe we are here to help the less fortunate students; those who have struggled, and those who may not be *ready* for college-level work.

As part of my research on Embedded Community Colleges, I interviewed a dean of math and sciences at Bridge and Buffer Community College (pseudonym for confidentiality purposes). His efforts to reform developmental education were truly astounding and innovative. Like many other leaders in the areas of math and science, he felt pressure to increase activities in the areas of STEM (science, technology, engineering, and math). Creating an engineering program that articulated with the state universities was not an easy task. After months of negotiations, both with instructional staff and support services staff, the engineering program was born. However, he realized his focus had been on the STEM finish line the whole time. Students at the start of the STEM race were struggling just to reach college-level mathematics.

First, he discovered problems with the placement test, which was placing 95 percent of incoming freshman below college-level math. Next, he implemented a waiver system whereby students could sign a waiver bypassing the developmental courses. He found that over 70 percent of those who signed that waiver were successful in their college-level courses. To manage the remaining 30 percent, he created a self-paced system in which students passed a series of modules designed to provide the skills to take college-level math. The self-paced module system has resulted in a faster path through the developmental math program at this college.

Communities and their economies rely heavily on community colleges, especially during times of economic trouble.

The dean also asked me to consider the origins of developmental education and how it has strayed from the original purpose of educating returning adults who have been away from an academic setting for an extended period of time. Today, remedial or developmental education is at the heart of what we do at community colleges across the country. It speaks to the commitment we have to our students, our open-access mission, and our overall resilience as institutions of higher education.

Economic Impact

Communities and their economies rely heavily on community colleges, especially during times of economic trouble. Community colleges are positioned to train students quickly (faster than their university counterparts) through year-long (or less) certificate programs and more in-depth associate's degree programs. Direct-employment programs at community colleges prepare workers for the automotive industry (mechanics and auto body techs), medical industry (nurses and other technicians), welding industry (certified welders), and construction industry (plumbers, electricians, carpenters), to name just a few.

For every 1 percent increase in unemployment, community college enrollment can be expected to increase by 4 percent.

In an article published in *The Journal of Human Resources* in 1995[10], Julian Betts and Laurel McFarland demonstrated that for every 1 percent increase in unemployment, community college enrollment can be expected to increase by 4 percent. As leaders, we witnessed this during this most recent recession ("The Great Recession") as students flocked to community colleges in droves, many after losing their jobs. Community colleges were there when the national economy needed them most.

The importance of community colleges became even clearer to me as I traveled in support of my dissertation research. I learned that in many rural areas one need only mention "the college" and everyone knows you're referring to the local

---

10 Betts, Julian R., and Laurel L. McFarland. "Safe port in a storm: The impact of labor market conditions on community college enrollments." Journal of Human Resources (1995): 741-765.

community college. These rural community colleges enjoy a unique strategic position in their communities because they employ large numbers of respected professionals, credential various professions, and impact a wide variety of other organizations through partnerships and symbiotic relationships. These rural community colleges are likely to be what I refer to as Embedded Community Colleges, deeply connected to their local communities and important (sometimes, *essential*) economic contributors.

These rural community colleges are likely to be what I refer to as Embedded Community Colleges, deeply connected to their local communities and important (sometimes, *essential*) economic contributors.

As state support of higher education continues to recede, we see community colleges taking their economic case to the media and to people in their service areas. In February of 2014, the American Association of Community Colleges (http://www.aacc.nche.edu) released a report in partnership with Economic Modeling Specialists (referenced earlier) titled "Where Value Meets Values: The Economic Impact of Community Colleges." The highlight of the report is that for every dollar invested in community colleges, taxpayers can expect to receive $7 in benefits. The report showed that community colleges educate 11.6 million students annually and contribute $809 billion to the nation's gross domestic product (5.4 percent of $15.1 trillion) not only through direct expenditures, but also through indirect impacts, such as the increased earnings of its graduates.

In 2012, Dr. Nancy McCallin, president of the Colorado Community College system, commissioned a study by Economic Modeling Specialists that showed the economic impact of the system's thirteen community colleges was around $3 billion. The study also showed that of the $107 million allocated to community colleges by the state of Colorado, taxpayers can expect a return of approximately $182 million.

In 2010, the Texas Association of Community Colleges commissioned a study by (yes, you guessed it) Economic Modeling Specialists that measured the economic impact of Texas community colleges to be $1.6 billion, with a $28.7 billion contribution over the last 30 years.

In 2011, an economic impact study by the state of Connecticut showed data similar to other states. Taxpayers could expect a return of $350 million on their $199 million investment in community colleges. In addition to all the income benefits students enjoy, the study cited an increase in tax receipt returns of 14 percent due to community college activities.

The positive economic impact of community colleges on our national economy and our local economies is profound and can be felt both directly (direct expenditures) and indirectly (increased earnings and increased tax receipts).

The relationships we establish and maintain with our community stakeholders are absolutely essential strategic efforts and will ensure our enduring success as institutions that credential future professionals. Our economic impact isn't tied only to what we spend and how we spend it in our communities; our impact is also connected to the strategic decisions we make within our local economies.

As a community college leader, chances are you work with a number of different stakeholders, each exerting different types of pressure on you and your institution. The local builders association may want your college to offer a new program in green/sustainable construction. You may be pressured by a nearby military installation to offer course credit for military training. Local utilities may ask you to provide linemen or power plant technician courses. And the list goes on. The relationships and the strategic decisions attached to those relationships will impact the economic welfare of the community you serve.

Crystal Ball Community College (one of the sites in my study) developed an innovative approach to serving the economic needs of its community by practicing what I refer to as Predictive

Program Development. We often hear that we're preparing our students for jobs that don't yet exist, and CBCC is doing just that. Rather than waiting to see what industries develop in the surrounding area, CBCC took a predictive strategic direction. They predict what industries will materialize in the local county, and then they invest in academic programs to meet those needs. Recently, CBCC invested time and money to develop a new applied engineering program designed to satisfy the needs of potential industries. This innovative school also improved its construction program and invested $5 million to build a career technical education center to support the new applied engineering program, the welding program, and an improved construction program.

> The innovative and distinctive decisions you make as a community college leader *can and will* affect the strategic direction of your institution.

As we look toward the future, community colleges will continue to play an important role in our economy and will continue providing opportunities for our students. The innovative and distinctive decisions you make as a community college leader *can and will* affect the strategic direction of your institution. By understanding the impact of community colleges on our students, our communities, and our economy, you are positioned to facilitate success that will define community colleges well into the future.

Chapter 2

The Deeply-Held Identity
of Community Colleges

*T*he title of this chapter implies that a collective identity exists among the 1,100 or so community colleges across the United States. Although each institution has a unique identity, modern community colleges are far more alike than they are different. This is due primarily to a phenomenon that plagues institutions of higher education.

Labeled **isomorphism,** this phenomenon is identified in the work of Paul DiMaggio and Walter Powell[11], researchers who studied how organizations behave and what types of forces influence their activities and those of their representatives.

DiMaggio and Powell identified three types of isomorphism: **coercive isomorphism, mimetic isomorphism,** and **normative isomorphism.** Please bear with me as I present a technical, but extremely important, explanation of these concepts. This knowledge is a vital part of understanding how to plan and implement successful strategic efforts for today's community colleges.

[11] DiMaggio, Paul J., and Walter W. Powell. "The iron cage revisited: Institutional isomorphism and collective rationality in organizational fields." *American Sociological Review* (1983): 147-160.

Coercive isomorphism occurs as the result of pressure from external organizations, such as governments, high schools, colleges, and universities. Each college must legitimize itself and find a niche—a strategic position within higher education. This means conforming to demands and mandates from other entities.

Mimetic isomorphism mirrors the activities and behaviors of other institutions, usually in areas associated with uncertainty. An example of this might be exploring new programs based on their perceived success at other community colleges.

Normative isomorphism typically results from influences associated with professionalism, such as when an institution adopts practices or policies learned through best practices conferences, professional associations, and union-related activities.

> We have a collective identity; a shared set of beliefs and a common ideology that drives our decisions as community college leaders.

Considered as a whole, the nation's community colleges have more in common than we have differences. Just one visit to another community college should convince you of that. I will discuss this phenomenon in later chapters, but for now it's important to understand that as community colleges, we have a collective identity; a shared set of beliefs and a common ideology that drives our decisions as community college leaders.

A Story

In May of 2006, I participated in my first graduation ceremony as a member of the faculty at Cochise College. I was proud that I'd survived my first year as a college professor and thankful for finding a career I loved. Teaching was fun, rewarding, and most importantly, it made me happy. I knew I wanted to do this for the rest of my professional life. I still feel that way.

The first graduation ceremony had an unexpected emotional impact on me. This was the first time I'd attended a graduation with fewer than a thousand graduates, plus thousands more people in the audience. That ceremony on the Douglas campus of Cochise College took me by surprise. The city of Douglas sits on the Arizona-Mexico border in southeastern Arizona and boasts a population of approximately 17,000. According to the U.S. Census Bureau, the median household income is $28,548 compared to the Arizona average of $50,256. Eighty two percent of Douglas residents are Hispanic and 73 percent speak Spanish as their primary language at home. Over 60 percent of Douglas High School students attend Cochise College after graduation, but many lack the level of academic preparation necessary to find immediate success. Having taught full-time on the Douglas campus for three years, I can tell you this doesn't stop them. Douglas campus students are resilient. With the help of support programs like the TRIO program referenced in Chapter One, they wade through remedial math and English courses and on through their college-level coursework. They struggle, but they persist, and graduation is a huge accomplishment. For many students on the Douglas campus of Cochise College, this would be their last graduation ceremony. Few go on to complete a bachelor's degree. Most are content with an associate's degree and will find stable employment locally to be close to family and friends. For most, this commencement ceremony represented years of work (two-year college it was not) and countless late-night study sessions.

Yet, there they sat, on metal folding chairs on the large grassy field outside the Charles Di Peso library, in their graduation gowns, waiting for the college president to hand them their degrees. Statistically, they shouldn't have even been there (see upcoming section titled Factors Contributing to Success).

These are all aspects of the community college environment that I failed to understand after my first year as a member of the faculty at Cochise College. Community colleges are designed to lift up the underdog, to provide supports to those less fortunate, and improve the lives of those in our society who need it most. We hold the community college mission close to our hearts and use that purpose to drive us as community college leaders.

I know how strange this next sentence is going to sound and I'm willing to take all the inevitable teasing and ridicule, but here goes: Pomp and Circumstance is one of my favorite songs. It gives me goose bumps every time. There I said it. Fortunately, I get to hear it at least once a year, and no I do not have it on my iPod . . . yet.

> We hold the community college mission close to our hearts and use that purpose to drive us as community college leaders.

No more than 300 graduates participated in the ceremony on that spring day, but you could have fooled me. The crowd of family and friends was enormous and loud—and they did not disappoint. Each graduate was cheered loudly, accompanied by the occasional obnoxious noise makers (typically heard at sporting events) that helped keep older members of the faculty awake (sorry!). The crowd was electric and the graduates beamed with pride upon receiving their diplomas from our president. I was excited for all of them and for their bright futures. Cochise College allows for one or more student speakers at graduation, and this year's speaker exemplified the mission and identity of community colleges. Her name was Heather Morrison. Heather had fled an abusive, alcoholic husband in North Carolina to start a new life for herself and her sons. This new life began at a homeless shelter called the Women's Transition Project in Bisbee, Arizona, just a twenty minute drive to the Douglas campus of Cochise College. Heather decided to enroll as a full-time student at Cochise, continued to contribute to the shelter in different ways, majored in physics, maintained a 4.0 grade point average, and was named to the all-Arizona academic first team, which meant she was one of the top 22 community college students in the state and would receive a tuition waiver to complete her bachelor's degree at one of the three public state universities. Additionally, she earned the prestigious Jack Kent Cooke Foundation scholarship which amounted to another $30,000 per year. Only 25 community college transfer students in the *nation* earned that distinction in 2006. Heather was an amazing student with a moving story of resilience, perseverance, and eventual triumph.

Realistically, not all our students can be Heather Morrison, but try telling that to our faculty and staff. We understand our open-access mission. We understand the struggles our students have faced in their lives. We believe in their aspirations and we're committed to providing instruction and support to help them succeed in higher education. As community college leaders, it's important that we understand this modern identity of community colleges and how that identity developed.

This chapter about the collective identity of community colleges serves two purposes. First, it will allow you to better understand the history and identity of community colleges and what drives our community college leaders to adhere to that identity.

Second, it will contextualize one of the most fascinating findings of my research. This finding relates to the decisions of community college leaders who were faced with reduced financial resources. Did they panic? They did not. Did they frantically seek alternative revenue streams that would alter the identity of their institutions? They did not. When faced with reductions, did they drastically raise tuition for their already struggling student population? They did not.

While these questions will be analyzed in greater detail in later chapters, it is important to understand the role of *identity* and how that identity might influence your decisions as an innovative community college leader. This chapter serves to inform future chapters on reduced state allocations, fiscal constraint, the community college ecosystem, and of course, community college strategy. As you will learn in these future chapters, when times are tough, when the cycle of reductions seem endless and the barrage of external pressures increases, these leaders are guided by the open-access mission of community colleges to serve their communities and provide a path to success for a traditionally disadvantaged student population.

The Collective Identity of Community Colleges

Let's start by agreeing on what the collective identity of community colleges actually consists of, with a little help from the American Association of Community Colleges (http://www. aacc.nche.edu).

1. **Comprehensive:** Modern community colleges try to be all things to all people. Consequently, we offer a mind-boggling array of programs ranging from transfer-type courses like Math, English, Science, and Social Studies, to vocational or direct-employment programs like Welding Technology, Fire Science, or Automotive Technology. We also tend to offer a wide range of non-credit courses.

2. **Serve All Segments of Society:** We believe strongly in open-access admission policies that welcome any and all students who possess just one thing: aspirations for success.

3. **Community:** We believe in serving our local communities, in many cases as *the* dominant provider of higher education services in our areas. We believe in the connections and relationships we build with the various stakeholders of our local community organizations.

4. **Teaching and Learning:** We believe in our mission as educators. Education is our primary objective and our resources tend to be allocated accordingly. While our

comprehensive mission might mean we are involved in many different activities, teaching and learning are at the very core of our identity and will remain such.

I challenge you to find a school among the 1,100 community colleges in the United States that doesn't adhere to these four core components of our identity. These priorities define the collective identity of today's modern community colleges.

The Evolution of the Community College Identity

The development, growth, vocationalization, and identity of community colleges has been well-documented and debated by a number of researchers throughout the years. Steven Brint and Jerome Karabel's book titled *The Diverted Dream: Community Colleges and the Promise of Educational Opportunity in America, 1900-1985*[12] takes a critical look at the evolution of the community college mission over its 100 year history, from a transfer-focused mission to a mission that now includes both transfer and direct-employment programs. Kevin Dougherty's book titled *The Contradictory College*[13] takes another critical look at the history of community colleges by examining the role of various external forces on the growth of these institutions. Each of these scholars will be referenced in future sections.

Federal Government Influence

According to the American Association of Community Colleges (the primary advocacy association for community colleges) there are approximately 1,100 community colleges across the U.S. Considering the first community college was

---

12 Brint, Steven, and Jerome Karabel. *The Diverted Dream: Community Colleges and the Promise of Educational Opportunity in America, 1900-1985.* Oxford University Press, Inc., 200 Madison Ave., New York, NY 10016, 1989.

13 Dougherty, Kevin J. *The contradictory college: The conflicting origins, impacts, and futures of the community college.* SUNY Press, 1994.

founded in 1901, this means an average of ten new community colleges have opened every year since then. In reality, the growth of community colleges resembles a bell curve and was heavily influenced by federal government policy and legislation from 1944 to 1965. In 1946, President Harry Truman commissioned a report titled "Higher Education for American Democracy" that served to increase the federal government's role in community college expansion. The G.I. bill had been passed in 1944, exponentially increasing access to higher education for the millions of servicemen and women returning from WWII.

Community colleges were there when the country needed them most, retraining the masses and providing pathways to success for professionals in a number of industries.

Next, President Lyndon Johnson reaffirmed the nation's commitment to higher education by signing the Higher Education Act of 1965 into law. These pieces of legislation, along with the wave of returning members of our military, resulted in a massive expansion of community colleges. Again, community colleges were there when the country needed them most, retraining the masses and providing pathways to success for professionals in a number of industries.

The Comprehensive (and Expanding) Mission of Community Colleges

Scholars tend to agree that many factors led to the current identity of community colleges as comprehensive, open-access institutions. Student influences, industry pressures, and legislative forces played a role in crafting the identity of the modern U.S. community college.

However, the mission and identity of community colleges has changed since Joliet Junior College was founded in Illinois in 1901. For the first fifty years, the community college system primarily served students seeking liberal arts transfer courses.

This is where the term "junior college" originated. Over the next thirty years, community colleges slowly modified their strategic position to become open-access institutions that included vocational education designed to prepare students for employment. By 1980, the "vocationalization" of community colleges was complete, with the clear majority of students in direct-employment vocational programs.

As I mentioned in Chapter One, all community colleges now have a mix of transfer versus direct-employment programs. Strategically successful community colleges adjust the proportion of those offerings to meet the needs of their student population. Some institutions might focus more on direct-employment programs while others may have close relationships with a nearby four-year university, resulting in a greater focus on transfer programs. As an innovative leader, I challenge you to examine the mix of offerings at your institution and determine whether it is appropriate for the community you serve. Are industry representatives exerting a disproportionate influence on your offerings? Are your state universities guilty of the same?

Understanding why the vocationalization of community colleges occurred has led to considerable academic debate. Scholars generally agree it results from a variety of influences. Brint and Karabel[14], borrowing from economic theory, contend the migration toward vocational education may have occurred primarily due to the influence of two groups of stakeholders: our students and private industry. First, their **consumer-choice model** indicates that student demand and choices based on efficiency resulted in growth and vocationalization. The consumer-choice model suggests that students choose a community college education because it's cheaper and they get more "bang-for-the-buck." With community college tuition

---

14 Brint, Steven, and Jerome Karabel. "Institutional origins and transformations: The case of American community colleges." *The new institutionalism in organizational analysis* 337 (1991): 360.

still a fraction of the cost for university tuition, we certainly understand this theory. Consider too, that community colleges have shown a commitment to keeping tuition low, whereas our university counterparts show no such commitment. Second, Brint and Karabel's **business-domination** model says that private industry plays a large role in affecting curriculum and determining course and program offerings at community colleges.

> We have evolved somewhat from that subservient strategic position. We are no longer rooted in place between our K-12 and university education partners.

Noted scholars Samuel Bowles and Herbert Gintis[15] argue that community colleges have been purposefully subordinated into the role of junior colleges by the elite, high-socioeconomic class in the U.S. This subordination seems to have contributed to the subservient strategic position of community colleges where they were prevented from training future upper class professionals (doctors, lawyers, engineers) and forced to train members of the working class

We have evolved somewhat from that subservient strategic position. We are no longer rooted in place between our K-12 and university education partners. I wonder what Bowles and Gintis make of institutions like Seattle Central College, South Seattle College and North Seattle College? All three community colleges dropped the word "community" from their names, based largely on their ability to now offer bachelor's degrees; a clear encroachment on the traditionally elevated strategic position of universities. What might Bowles and Gintis make of the fact that, as of 2014, twenty-one states allow their community colleges to award bachelor's degrees? Florida alone has twenty-two community colleges that offer bachelor's

---

15 Bowles, Samuel, and Herbert Gintis. *Schooling in capitalist America.* Vol. 57. New York: Basic Books, 1976.

degrees in business, nursing, and education. Washington has eleven community colleges offering bachelor's degrees. In 2013, legislators in Michigan passed a law (opposed by the state universities) that allows community colleges to offer bachelor's degree programs, making it the 21st state to do so. If legislators have their way in California, its 112 community colleges will offer an applied bachelor's degree in the near future. However, it's important to note that most bachelor's degrees being offered by community colleges are categorized as "workforce" degrees or extensions of popular direct-employment associate's degree programs.

Influence of State and Local Governments

Drawing upon research from community college systems in five states, the prolific higher education scholar Kevin Dougherty contends that state and local government officials (legislators, school superintendents, high school principals, school board members, etc.) played an extraordinary role in the development and vocationalization of community colleges. Dougherty's **state relative autonomy perspective**[16] argues that policymakers often use their influence to shape the strategic direction of the community college system, whether it be to maintain the prestige of four-year institutions, fiscal constraint issues, or simply self-interest and political gain. I will revisit this concept in Chapter Four when we take a closer look at the forces that exert pressure on community colleges.

Think Different (thanks, Steve Jobs)

In 2008, I was asked to make a presentation to a cohort of leaders at Cochise College. The members of the cohort were participating in a series of training sessions as a professional

---

16 Dougherty, Kevin. "Educational policy-making and the relative autonomy of the state: The case of occupational education in the community college." *In Sociological Forum*, vol. 3, no. 3, pp. 400-432. Kluwer Academic Publishers, 1988.

development initiative called the Leadership Academy. I had just taken a class titled Strategic Positioning in Higher Education by one of my mentors, who is among the most respected scholars in the field of higher education research—Gary Rhoades with the University of Arizona's Center for the Study of Higher Education. As evidence of his national acclaim, Dr. Rhoades would soon take a leave of absence from the university to serve as the general secretary for the American Association of University Professors.

> Truly innovative institutions find strategic niches by paying close attention to the needs of their unique communities.

The central concept of Gary Rhoades' course was one I introduced near the beginning of this chapter: **isomorphism, or** the phenomenon of organizations behaving similarly to one another for a variety of reasons (some internal and some external). My research in this area is heavily influenced by Gary's research and writings[17]. He speaks about making distinctive strategic choices that challenge the status quo; choices that take advantage of unique opportunities at your college or university.

In my presentation to the group of leaders, I introduced the concept of normative isomorphism and tied it to the concept of "best practices." Since many of these leaders had visited other community colleges, I asked them a series of rhetorical questions designed to challenge their strategic mindsets. I asked them to think about the last community college they visited. Did the school have a continuing education center that taught non-credit classes? All nodded. Did they have an open-admissions policy? Everyone nodded. Did they have a visible career technical education or vocational program? All heads nodded. Did they have a developmental education initiative

---

[17] Rhoades, Gary. "Distinctive choices in intersecting markets: Seeking strategic niches." *Future of the American public research university* (2007): 121-143.

underway? Yes. Did they all offer online courses? All nodded. And the list went on and on. My point to the cohort was that, as future leaders, they needed to fight the urge to behave similarly to other institutions.

Isomorphism is the enemy of innovation. Truly innovative institutions find strategic niches (as promoted by Gary Rhoades) by paying close attention to the needs of their unique communities. While we, as institutions, tend toward similarity, strategically successful community colleges initiate programs to satisfy the *unique* needs of their communities.

- Cochise College has a strong strategic relationship with Ft. Huachuca whereby soldiers receive college credit for the majority of their military training.
- Estrella Mountain Community College has an excellent program in Power Plant Technology and Safety due in large part to its relationship with the nearby Palo Verde Nuclear Generating Station which is one of the largest nuclear power plants in the U.S.
- The University of Hawaii Community College System boasts a strong program in hotel and tourism management and a world-class marine biology program.
- The Community and Technical College System of West Virginia has a thriving Mining Technology and Energy Technologies program that meets the need of its equally thriving mining industry.

As a leader, it's so easy to make safe decisions. We're encouraged to always implement initiative XYZ because it worked well at another school. Such decisions may be easy, but they rarely affect the strategic direction of the institution. I ended my presentation with a 1997 Apple television ad titled "Here's to the Crazy Ones" with Steve Jobs narrating:

"The misfits. The rebels. The troublemakers. The round pegs in the square holes. The ones who see things differently...They have no respect for the status quo . . .While some see them as the crazy ones, we see genius." The ad included images of Albert Einstein, Bob Dylan, Martin Luther King, Jr., John Lennon, Muhammad Ali, Mahatma Gandhi, Pablo Picasso, and more.

As innovative leaders, I challenge you to recognize isomorphism when you see it. I challenge you to think differently, to be unique, to implement initiatives that respond to the singular needs of your community. By doing so, you will define yourself as an innovative leader and will have an enormous strategic impact on your institution.

> As innovative leaders, I challenge you to recognize isomorphism when you see it. I challenge you to think differently, to be unique, to implement initiatives that respond to the singular needs of your community.

As we begin looking at the community college ecosystem, the divestment of state governments, and the strategic activities of community college leaders, I ask you to begin considering the external forces that exert pressure on community colleges. These forces have the potential to impact the strategic direction of colleges across the country and will affect our decisions as innovative leaders.

Chapter 3

*The Great State Divestment
in Higher Education*

*I*had just returned from Crystal Ball Community College after completing a second series of interviews for my dissertation research. Thoughts bounced around my brain like lottery balls. This was a Wednesday, which meant I'd be driving forty-five minutes to teach two classes on the Douglas campus of Cochise College, something I had done for the past nine years. While others might see this trek as a burden, I consider it an opportunity to reflect, ponder, and unwind. As I drove that day, I sorted out my thoughts.

One of my interviewees mentioned that the divestment of state government in community colleges made no sense and was, in fact, the complete opposite of what should be happening. Instead of cutting funds, states should offer *more* resources during tough economic times.

The nation had just started to slip into a deep recession, largely due to the housing bubble. History and research both indicated that displaced workers would soon flock to community colleges. And they did. To further assist the record numbers of unemployed across the country, President Obama and Congress had recently passed the American Recovery and Reinvestment Act of 2009, which would infuse $800 billion into federal, state, and local economies through infrastructure and education initiatives designed to retrain people and get them back to work. Community colleges served a central role in the country's economic recovery. I witnessed this first-hand as Cochise College experienced record enrollments

While the federal government's commitment to the overall economic recovery was commendable, the declining support of state governments to community colleges was deplorable.

According to Christopher Mullin and Kent Phillippe in a report prepared for the AACC, community college enrollments grew 21.8 percent between 2007 and 2011. Community colleges welcomed the masses with open arms, training nurses, computer technicians, automotive technicians, welders, construction workers, and more. While the federal government's commitment to the overall economic recovery was commendable, the declining support of state governments to community colleges was deplorable. At a time when state allocations to community colleges should have increased to help these schools handle increased enrollment, state governments across the nation proceeded to *reduce* their allocations in an attempt to protect other government-funded services. According to a report by the American Council on Education titled "State Funding: A Race to the Bottom," 48 out of 50 states decreased their allocations to institutions of higher education from 1980 to 2011. Only Wyoming and North Dakota managed to maintain their financial commitment to higher education at +2.3 percent and +0.8 percent respectively from 1980 through 2011.

In 1979, Randy VanWarmer came out with a song written after a heart-wrenching breakup with his girlfriend six months earlier. The soft, 80s love song rocketed up the charts worldwide and seem to epitomize music from that decade; soft, slow, and emotional. When I listen to "Just When I Needed You Most" these days, I think not about lost love and heartbreak, but of community colleges. Yes, I am so immersed in my research that I relate the emotional suffering of 80s love songs to the fiscal crisis community colleges face today.

"You packed in the morning, I stared out the window and I struggled for something to say. You left in the rain without closing the door. I didn't stand in your way."

At a recent presentation to a room full of community college leaders, I asked the question "How many of you are *NOT* currently managing budget cuts or state allocation reductions?" Silence. Crickets chirping. Not a single person in that room of 75 people from community colleges around the country could raise a hand. All were seeing reductions to their state allocations. All were struggling to find innovative ways to meet the needs of their students and communities with fewer resources from state governments.

This chapter is about the divestment of state governments in higher education.

> At a recent presentation to a room full of community college leaders, I asked the question "How many of you are *NOT* currently managing budget cuts or state allocation reductions?" Silence. Crickets chirping.

As we look at the ongoing, seemingly never-ending decline in state allocations to community colleges, I will introduce concepts to be discussed in future chapters. These concepts deal with how community college leaders have responded to this divestment and speaks to the heart of my research agenda which is "How do we, as community college leaders, facilitate innovation and strategic behavior despite reduced financial resources?"

This chapter contains three sections. First, I look at the overall divestment of state governments in higher education. In this section, I will show how state governments have purposefully and systematically withdrawn support from public community colleges and universities. The last two sections show how these two different entities have managed the divestment. Universities typically lean toward program cuts, drastic tuition increases, and alternative revenue streams (endowment fundraising and partnerships with private industry), while community colleges have fought the urge to transfer that financial burden to already disadvantaged student populations.

As innovative leaders, it's important we understand the financial pressures community colleges experience. The second half of this book will closely examine different strategies to neutralize external pressure and manage fiscal crisis while remaining strategically successful.

The Great Divestment

Institutions of higher education face a fiscal crisis. This we can all agree on. How we handle this crisis will define us in the future and may even alter the identity of our respective institutions. As state support continues to decline, we're forced to make tough decisions related to our institutional priorities, alternative revenue streams, partnerships with private industry, and our overall strategic position in higher education.

The crisis we face is a bit more complicated than states simply allocating fewer dollars to higher education. While these cuts have been consistent over the years, part of our frustration as higher education leaders lies with the creative and often unpredictable ways state governments reduce their financial commitment to higher education. Pools of money that had long been considered untouchable by state government are now being swept up by states and allocated elsewhere.

Statutes that govern funding to community colleges by a rigid formula are being ignored and not funded. The creative nature of these cuts, coupled with the misinformation or downright deceptive practices of state governments and state legislatures regarding higher education funding, adds new challenges to the job of higher education leaders. We ask ourselves:

- How deep will our budget cuts go this year?
- How will the cuts affect new positions at the school?
- When will the legislature finalize its budget?
- Will drastic tuition increases be necessary?
- Will we rely heavily on our foundation to replace lost revenues?
- Will there be more emphasis on lucrative industry partnerships?
- Will technology transfer activities take priority over other initiatives?
- Will this result in a hiring freeze or a hiring chill?
- Why did the governor's office ask for budget documents, and then use those documents to justify further cuts?

We see the trend toward zero state allocations, and already some institutions are planning for this possibility. As a community college president said to me "At what point do we stop answering the phone?" A rhetorical question to be sure, but with state allocations to his institution reduced to three to five percent of its total budget, the question deserves deep consideration.

In an article titled "The Policy Shift in State Financial Aid Programs" in 2002[18], Donald Heller of Michigan State University noted that from 1969 to 1995, state appropriations decreased as a percentage of overall state government expenditures. He was one of the first researchers to demonstrate that states tend to reduce higher education appropriations during tough economic times and increase them during healthy economic times. He

---

18 Heller, Donald E. "The policy shift in state financial aid programs." In *Higher education: Handbook of theory and research,* pp. 221-261. Springer Netherlands, 2002.

also published data showing that tuition and fees now account for a larger percentage of expenditures than ever before.

We are experiencing *The Great Divestment* in higher education. Sadly, this divestment has occurred over the last three or four decades. According to the previously referenced report from the American Council on Education ("State Funding: A Race to the Bottom"), the downward trend of state allocations to public institutions is expected to hit zero for many states between 2030 and 2050.

> We are experiencing *The Great Divestment* in higher education. Sadly, this divestment has occurred over the last three or four decades.

In 1975, state and local governments spent 60 percent of their budgets on public higher education. In 2010, this number was down to 34 percent. Recall that only two of the fifty states can claim to have increased their allocations to higher education from 1980 to 2011 (Wyoming and North Dakota). Between 1980 and 2011, Arizona reduced its appropriations to higher education by 61.9 percent. Other states followed suit:

Oregon, 61.5%.
Rhode Island, 62.1%.
South Carolina, 66.8%.
Colorado, 69.4%.
Minnesota, 55.8%.
Virginia, 53.6%.
Vermont, 51.3%.

Many community college leaders fully expect their allocations to disappear. The question those leaders should be asking is, "What will we do then?"

According to a 2013 report by Phil Oliff, Vincent Palacios, Ingrid Johnson, and Michael Leachman for the Center for Budget and Policy Priorities, between 2008 and 2013, states spent 28 percent less per student…"just when we needed them most" (height of the recession). The authors share that eleven states cut per student funding by over 33 percent. Thirty-six states have cut per student spending by over 20 percent and Arizona and New Hampshire cut their per student spending by 50 percent. Again, we see the shining stars of Wyoming and North Dakota with per student increases of 7.5 percent and 16.5 percent respectively. Where does your state rank? See http:// www.cbpp.org/.

During The Great Recession, states overwhelmingly chose drastic spending cuts over increasing revenues through taxes and fees for government services. As higher education leaders are well-aware, colleges and universities are great at starting programs, but terrible at ending programs. We are good at building and horrible at demolition; quick to expand, but slow when it comes to contraction. While some community colleges chose to reduce administrative costs and aggressively cut all the low hanging excess fruit, most schools were still in the position of needing to increase revenue (tuition and property tax increases) to make ends meet in the short-term and to build financial reserves that would help guard against future drastic cuts.

Lawmakers believe that community colleges and universities can sustain themselves regardless of the economy. This might explain the comment of one of the presidents in my study when he said "Community Colleges have been their own worst enemy. Whatever state government cuts, we just make do. We find a way to get it done. We have always found a way to just get it done."

In 2004, Bruce Johnstone published an article in the *Economics of Education Review*[19] using the economic concept of cost sharing to analyze the rationale for receding state support of higher education. He writes that the cost of higher education

---

19 Johnstone, D. Bruce. "The economics and politics of cost sharing in higher education: comparative perspectives." *Economics of education review* 23, no. 4 (2004): 403-410.

is typically the responsibility of four groups: governments, parents, students, and donors. He shows that the trend in the United States is clearly moving away from government, toward placing a greater burden on parents, students, and donors.

Those who run state governments now realize, after reductions dating back to 1980, that colleges and universities are resilient. We find a way to plug the holes. We find a way to get it done. We find a way to replace lost revenue, although this can cause a strained relationship with state governments when they disagree with drastic tuition increases.

We create reserve accounts.

We partner with private industry.

We initiate fundraising campaigns.

Resilience is a part of our identity. We see it in our students and they inspire us to overcome our institutional adversities.

In the following sections we will look at how universities and community colleges respond to state divestment, in the past and the present. You will see a wide range of reactions; some good, some bad; some strategic, some harmful. As an innovative community college leader, I hope you will recognize the damage caused by the harmful reactions and be inspired by the inclusiveness of positive strategies.

University Response to The Great Divestment

According to the U.S. Department of Labor, from 2003 to 2013, tuition at public four-year universities increased by 79.5 percent. This was higher than any other cost category, including medical care, food and beverages, housing, clothing, and the overall consumer price index at 26.7 percent.

According to a report by the Center for Budget and Policy Priorities, from 2008-2013 (The Great Recession), public universities increased tuition an average of 27 percent while in Arizona and California, public university tuition increased by approximately 70 percent.

As state support of higher education declines, universities have no problem placing more of the cost sharing burden on students and their families. At my alma mater, the University of Arizona, the current cost of one in-state undergraduate unit is $764 ($671 for tuition and $93 in fees). That puts the annual cost of full-time enrollment (30 units) at $22,920. Compare that to Cochise College, where I work. Tuition is $73 per in-state unit, for an annual cost of $2,190.

I'm always flattered when an organization takes an interest in my research, especially if that organization is not a community college or university. This was certainly the case when a member of the Sierra Vista City Council asked me to give a presentation on community college strategy and strategic partnerships to support the council's educational strategic priorities. I happily accepted, but informed the council member that my presentation featured pessimism before presenting optimism. The first part of my presentation is always difficult to hear because it contains much of what I'm discussing in this chapter surrounding *The Great Divestment*.

> Affordable tuition is a clear, strategic choice by an administration that *refuses* to transfer the financial burden to students.

As I relayed the evidence of this great divestment in higher education, many of the council members shook their heads in disappointment. In conversations with some of them after the meeting, they thanked me for enlightening them and expressed disappointment in state governments. They agreed the policies were counterintuitive and also agreed that the long-term strategic success of community colleges should include greater emphasis on becoming "embedded community colleges" (see Chapter 5).

Universities do not have the same deeply-held identity that community colleges hold so dear. I discussed this identity with the city council and explained why Cochise College tuition remained low. Affordable tuition is a clear, strategic choice by an administration that *refuses* to transfer the financial burden to students. Community college students can pay an entire year's worth of tuition and books with the federal need-based Pell grant of around $5,000. This $5,000 just doesn't cut it at a university.

In addition to drastic tuition increases, many universities have started aligning themselves with private industry in a phenomenon called "academic capitalism." In 1997, Sheila Slaughter and Larry Leslie of the Center for the Study of Higher Education at the University of Arizona pioneered the theory of academic capitalism by recognizing the growing closeness of the market and institutions of higher education. In their book titled "Academic Capitalism: Politics, Policies, and the Entrepreneurial University,"[20] the authors demonstrate that many institutions are aligning themselves closer to the market as a way to generate new revenue streams or replace dwindling revenue streams. In 2004, Sheila Slaughter and Gary Rhoades offered an updated definition of academic capitalism in their book "Academic Capitalism and the New Economy."[21] They argued this new definition should include an institution's behaviors relative to the new information/technology-based economy. Slaughter and Rhoades believed the definition of academic capitalism should be expanded to include the creation of relationships with new economy stakeholders.

This second book on academic capitalism focuses not on the encroachment of the industry into higher education, but rather the fact that the universities are already saturated with market-like behaviors and initiatives such as product

20 Slaughter, Sheila, and Larry L. Leslie. *Academic capitalism: Politics, policies, and the entrepreneurial university.* The Johns Hopkins University Press, 2715 North Charles Street, Baltimore, MD 21218-4319, 1997.

21 Slaughter, Sheila, and Gary Rhoades. *Academic capitalism and the new economy: Markets, state, and higher education.* JHU Press, 2004.

patents, development of products with commercial value, and technology transfer in advanced fields such as the STEM areas (Science, Technology, Engineering, Math).

My research shows that while academic capitalism is prevalent at universities, it's almost non-existent at community colleges. The primary reason is that universities have a strong research agenda, while most community colleges do not conduct research and therefore lack the synergy and potential for profitable technology transfers.

However, community colleges can—and do—leverage resources from external sources.

They partner when appropriate and share resources as necessary, but they usually don't look for external, for-profit revenue streams. Is that a disadvantage? Perhaps not. Researchers argue that academic capitalism tends to further disadvantage traditionally disadvantaged populations. The second academic capitalism book by Slaughter and Rhoades delves into the idea that academic capitalism may have a negative effect on student access to higher education. The authors document the historical access and struggles of poor students, minorities, and women in higher education.

As discussed earlier in this chapter, we know that during hard economic times, universities tend to shift the burden to students and their families by raising tuition. This might be compared to a business raising consumer prices when production costs go up. Academic capitalism encourages these schools to behave even more like businesses by developing a profit-driven, no-nonsense approach to solving financial problems.

What's the problem here? Universities are not businesses. Their goal is not profit. Their goal is quality educational services. Enormous danger is present when universities behave like businesses. They lose their heart. They risk their souls. They drift farther from their stated mission to educate, inspire, and provide educational opportunities to as many students as possible.

As an example, the academic capitalism authors (Leslie, Slaughter, and Rhoades) demonstrate that public universities have started to employ a "need conscious" approach to the admissions process. Students who can pay the full tuition price are admitted over students who are more academically qualified, but cannot pay the full tuition. The authors show that public universities are now targeting more "elite or moneyed segments of the student market" as a way to maximize tuition revenue.

I implore you to recognize that true innovation does not come from doing what every other school does or from duplicating something you're exposed to at a conference. True innovation comes from being different and finding new, exciting ways to provide educational services to your unique communities. True innovation comes from developing programs others wish to mirror, not the other way around.

> True innovation comes from developing programs others wish to mirror, not the other way around.

Also, keep in mind that raising tuition can lead to decreased enrollment, which negates the benefits of passing costs along to students and families. Research on this topic shows that indeed, tuition increases do negatively impact enrollment. Leslie and Brinkman (1987)[22] found that for every $100 increase in tuition, enrollments fall by 0.7 percent. Subsequent studies by Kane (1991)[23], McPherson (1978)[24], and Heller (1997)[25] put the range from -0.05 percent to -1.53 percent.

---

[22] Leslie, Larry L., and Paul T. Brinkman. "Student price response in higher education: The student demand studies." *The Journal of Higher Education* (1987): 181-204.

[23] Kane, Thomas J. "College entry by blacks since 1970: The role of college costs, family background, and the returns to education." *Journal of political Economy* (1994): 878-911.

[24] McPherson, Michael S. "The demand for higher education." *Public policy and private higher education* (1978): 143-196.

[25] Heller, Donald E. "Student price response in higher education: An update to Leslie and Brinkman." *Journal of higher education* (1997): 624-659.

Consider that full-time enrollment typically means a student is taking 30 units per academic year. For a community college, this $100 threshold is reached when per unit tuition is increased by $3.33. That means approximately 1 percent of that X percent decrease in enrollment could be attributed to an institution's recent tuition increases.

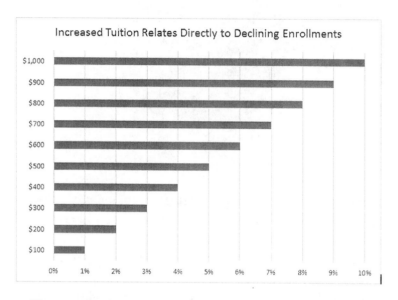

Increased Tuition Relates Directly to Declining Enrollments

Universities have no problem transferring the financial burden to students and their families. Let's take a look at what my research shows in terms of community college response to divestment.

Community College Response to Fiscal Pressures

Despite the ongoing divestment of state government, state appropriations remain a major source of revenue for community colleges. According to the American Association of Community Colleges, state funding accounts for 28 percent while local appropriations account for 17 percent and tuition and fees account for nearly 30 percent of revenue.

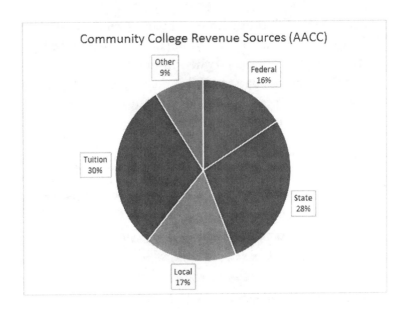

State government support matters to community colleges. Few of our beloved institutions can afford to ignore the phone calls of state government officials.

This section speaks to the heart of my study; how have we as community college leaders managed to find strategic success despite reduced financial resources? My goal in this section is to frame the issue by providing examples of how community colleges have responded to fiscal pressures in the past.

In a 2004 article published in *Change: The Magazine of Higher Learning*[26], longtime AACC President George R. Boggs notes that community colleges are facing a "perfect storm" of negative pressures. These pressures include reduced state allocations, aging leaders, rising costs, increased remediation needs of students, and economic pressures both national and local in many states. Dr. Boggs states...

---

26 Boggs, George R. 2004. "Community Colleges in a Perfect Storm." Change, Nov 6, 2004.

"At the same time that community colleges are faced with historic enrollment demands, they are struggling with severe budget cuts. Data from the Grapevines Project at Illinois State University found that state funding for public community colleges dropped by nearly $584.8 million between 2002-2003 and 2003-2004, with 22 states reporting decreased funding."

Dr. Boggs contends that community colleges are more sensitive to state allocation reductions because they receive 60 percent of their revenue from state and local funds compared to an average of 35 percent for public four-year institutions. How are community colleges coping?

He notes that community colleges have historically kept their tuition increases modest, but in 2002 and 2003 were shown to have raised tuition by 7.9 percent and 13.8 percent respectively. Community colleges have also implemented aggressive cost-cutting measures, including early retirement incentives, initiated reductions in force, and increased reliance on adjunct faculty (to the detriment of instructional quality).

Dr. Boggs states...

"When state finances are tight, higher education budgets are often cut disproportionately. To make matters worse, community colleges often absorb a disproportionate share of the higher education budget cuts. While funding policies vary by state, community colleges are the segment of higher education most reliant on public funding."

In a 1994 report titled "Broken Promises: The Impact of Budget Cuts and Fee Increases on the California Community Colleges,"[27] Jack McCurdy and William Trombley present findings of their study on the state of California's disinvestment in community colleges. The authors note several findings related to three straight years of reductions and budget cuts

---

27 McCurdy, Jack. "Broken Promises: The Impact of Budget Cuts and Fee Increases on the California Community Colleges." (1994).

to the California community college system. These findings include:

- raising student fees,
- laying off part-time instructors en masse,
- having to turn away 140,000 students,
- neglecting equipment and maintenance,
- cutbacks to build financial reserves,
- increased class size,
- and an overall decrease in instructional quality.

In an article published in the *Community College Review*[28] in 2003, Caroline Sheldon discusses the impact of "fiscal contraction" on community colleges and notes how state allocation reductions have negatively impacted student support services, thereby undermining the open-access mission of community colleges. She notes decreased access to instruction, declines in scheduled offerings, increases in the cost of attendance, and diminished funding for support services. Using the California Community College system as a case study, she argues that both access to and transfer from community colleges suffered because of budget cuts.

As community colleges continue facing reductions, their responses will impact their strategic position in higher education and have far-reaching effects on the landscape of higher education.

In the second half of this book, I present specific findings from my research and provide detailed recommendations. This final section of Chapter Three gives a preview of those findings and recommendations.

Preview of Key Strategies

The colleges in my study all used aggressive solutions to

---

[28] Sheldon, Caroline Q. "ERIC review: The impact of financial crises on access and support services in community colleges." *Community College Review* 31, no. 2 (2003): 73-90.

deal with state divestment. In some cases, they responded in proactive ways to neutralize the negative fiscal impact on their institutions. Three specific responses are worth mentioning in this chapter.

First, **accumulation of funds in financial reserve accounts** was a direct response to state government divestment. In order to provide a safety net, institutions in my study commonly maintained financial reserve account balances in excess of an entire year's budget. This gave them a sense of security—and the ability to continue strategic efforts despite receding state support. The sense of security came from knowing these reserve accounts would protect them against future cuts.

Second, the schools in my study did everything they could to **protect the core function of instruction.** Often, this meant cuts to support services, reductions in support positions, refusal to fill vacant support or administrative positions, and reductions in force to administration. Over all, each college aggressively insulated instruction from budget cuts.

Third, each site in my study **participated in a new strategic orientation,** moving away from relying on state government, toward a more symbiotic relationship with local community partners. These colleges experienced devastating effects from the drastic and sudden loss of state support. Their new orientation resulted in a more "embedded" relationship with local communities, thereby strengthening their strategic positions. In some cases, their new strategic orientations resulted in direct financial aid via bond initiatives or support for increased property taxes. In other cases support was more indirect, such as sharing resources, people, and expertise.

When I first presented the findings of my research to members of my dissertation committee at the Center for the Study of Higher Education at the University of Arizona, my findings were quite different from what's presented in this book, and also different from the final version of my dissertation. The committee pushed me to contextualize my results. For example,

I initially found that community colleges were transferring the financial burden to their students through tuition increases. In reality, these increases were modest compared to the drastic increases at four-year universities. My committee challenged me to adjust my perspective and see my findings in the greater context of higher education. I would be remiss not to recognize the members of my committee for shaping this first half of this book. I offer special thanks to those three distinguished scholars: Dr. Regina Deil-Amen, Dr. Ozan Jaquette, and Dr. Gary Rhoades.

Literary Intermission

*I*n the second half of this book I will make numerous references to my study that formed the foundation of my dissertation research. I thought it made sense to provide details about that study, its objectives, and its scope. Googling the sites in this study will return no results, as I substituted actual names for pseudonyms to protect the identities of my interviewees. The promise of confidentiality allowed these community college leaders to share openly with no fear of repercussions. On the flip side, my interview participants will find certain identifiable data has been modified to further protect their institution and identities. All of my interviewees have my eternal gratitude.

This section provides details of the three community college districts (Bridge and Buffer Community College, Grants and Reserves Community College, and Crystal Ball Community College) that served as the sites for my multi-site case study. These three sites were chosen partly because they were already dealing with their state's recent 50 percent reduction in appropriations to community college districts. This 50 percent reduction was devastating to all districts in the state, but these three schools responded proactively, immediately, and aggressively.

For example, Crystal Ball Community College reacted right away by slashing $1 million from its administration and immediately closing one of its centers. Bridge and Buffer Community College aggressively and successfully lobbied the state legislature three years after the state's drastic cuts to provide a new state-allocated revenue stream to all community colleges in the state. Grants and Reserves Community College brought in over $20 million in new grants in response to the state reductions.

Each site responded in a variety of ways, strategic and otherwise, to the 50 percent state funding cuts. Although each community college district differs in the amount of state aid they receive, all three schools are dealing with challenging and ongoing budgetary issues.

Bridge and Buffer Community College (**BBCC**) serves a rural student base in Bridge and Buffer County, with approximately 14,000 students enrolled in credit and non-credit courses across two main campuses and four remote centers. Twenty-six percent of its students transfer to a four-year university and the average student age is 31. This school operates on an approximately $40 million budget of which 30 percent comes from the state, 20 percent from tuition and fees, and 50 percent from local property taxes. A locally-elected governing board and president govern the college. Over the year, BBCC developed a close relationship with a local military installation and established a center on this installation, complete with academic and student support services. The college actively engages with external stakeholders through a variety of activities, including lobbying state government, K-12 partnerships, university partnerships, various industry connections, and creation of a statewide community college clearinghouse to better represent the interests of community colleges in the state.

Grants and Reserves Community College (**GRCC**) operates in a rural community and serves approximately 12,000 students. GRCC has ongoing partnerships with some of the state's universities to offer bachelors, masters, and doctoral degrees at their facilities. One of the state universities has maintained a permanent presence on campus for over two decades. The annual budget for GRCC is $35 million, of which 10 percent comes from the state, 30 percent from tuition and fees, and 60 percent from local property taxes. GRCC is governed by its locally-elected governing board and president. This college has two military installations within its service area and maintains strong relationships with both. The college has secured local bond and federal grant funding for a number of their recent strategic initiatives. These funds enable GRCC to participate in activities that would otherwise be financially out of reach. GRCC's financial reserves have served the same purpose.

Crystal Ball Community College (**CBCC**) serves approximately 10,000 students in two of the largest (square miles) and poorest counties in the state. This college operates on a $25 million budget, of which 30 percent comes from the state, 20 percent from tuition and fees, and 50 percent from local property taxes. Crystal Ball operates eight locations across two counties covering approximately 20,000 square miles. Maintaining these diverse locations proved inefficient in a number of ways. Consequently, CBCC has been forced to make difficult staffing decisions in the recent past and struggles to justify the distributed allocation of resources across these many locations. Of all community colleges in this state, CBCC had the swiftest response to budget cuts by making immediate reductions to administration, other reductions in force, closing a remote center, and other adjustments. This school doesn't claim significant industry players outside of government entities and utility companies, but has engaged in strategic projects in hopes of preparing students for potential employment within its service area.

Chapter 4

The Community College Ecosystem

The topic of "silos" has been widely discussed, debated, and largely derided by higher education researchers and practitioners alike. A silo segregates each unit or department of a school into a separate entity with its own resources and output. This separation has been condemned as a selfish strategic move that has negative effects on the parent institution.

Silos represent a myopic perspective, but they aren't formed with malicious intent. The silo effect is often a response to the specific requirements of a discipline, department, or program. For example, chemistry faculty around the U.S. can attest to the fact that the American Chemical Society exerts pressure regarding curriculum and methods of instructional delivery. Welders might attest to equal pressure from the American Welding Society. Accountants, nurses, and other professionals are required to pass industry-standard certification exams before they can find employment. Within these departments, it's easy to wear blinders and focus on one discipline rather than the entire college.

This discipline-loyal viewpoint may seem justified in the short term, but innovative leaders must learn to expand their perspectives. Doing so means peering over the sides of your silo to find potential synergies with other organizational units at your institution. This will make you a truly innovative leader. As you climb the ladder at your institution, initiatives you start by building bridges between departments will give you more influence and help you build a network of allies to call upon for future projects.

This chapter is about widening your perspective, understanding the entire community college ecosystem, and examining the forces that exert pressure on your institution. In addition, I will present the tools you need to manage or neutralize those negative pressures.

Challenging financial situations do have an upside. While dealing with budget cuts, the choices community colleges make are both difficult and illuminating. During times of turmoil, colleges reveal their true priorities and expose which activities truly define their institutional identities. This is an opportunity to clarify your goals and streamline your school.

> During times of turmoil, colleges reveal their true priorities and expose which activities truly define their institutional identities.

As innovative leaders, please understand that the second half of this book is meant to provide a roadmap for innovative and strategic success.

External Pressures and Identity

The strategic position of community colleges has evolved over the years from a system that primarily served transfer students, to a strategic position for providing vocational education, to the more comprehensive mission we see today.

Different researchers have explored pressures that helped shape the identity and strategic position of the modern community college. Some use economics to explain a student's choice of college. Others point to the role of private industry. Other researchers claim community colleges have been subordinated by society's upper class into roles as *junior* colleges, prohibited from providing elite education in areas such as law or medicine.

Noted higher education scholar Kevin Dougherty demonstrated that state government impacts the identity of community colleges by exerting self-serving legislative pressure. Scholars from Columbia University's Teachers College[29] (Gregory Anderson, Mariana Alfonso, and Jeffrey C. Sun) showed that legislative leaders conspired to move instruction to the community college level via statewide articulation agreements, because instruction is cheaper at theses colleges.

Quartering and Mandate

Helping a community college grow and thrive will be easier if you understand two concepts that provide a framework for analysis. First, the concept of *quartering community colleges* gives us a way to organize and explain pressures that influence community colleges.

Second, the concept of a *mandate to neutralize* highlights the importance of activities that manage the quartering pulls of external pressure. Institutions with a clear mandate to neutralize external forces have a greater capacity for strategic behavior and long-term success.

The Quartering of Community Colleges

Quartering is a new approach to understanding and managing pressures that grind away at community colleges. This concept divides influences into four general categories, with multiple pressures in each category. At any given time, a

[29] Anderson, Gregory, Mariana Alfonso, and Jeffrey Sun. "Rethinking cooling out at public community colleges: An examination of fiscal and demographic trends in higher education and the rise of statewide articulation agreements." The Teachers College Record 108, no. 3 (2006): 422-451.

community college may be actively managing pressures in all four categories; perhaps multiple pressures from each category. When your school or department is being pulled apart from various directions, the tendency is to focus on one "hot" issue at a time instead of taking a wider, more panoramic strategic view.

The key to managing these pressures is to identify each pressure point, determine its specific needs and requirements, and then form a strategy to neutralize each of those forces. For example, legislative pressures might lead you to analyze state laws and possibly hire a lobbyist to further your college's interests. Increased gasoline costs might lead to analyzing the use of school vehicles, perhaps finding a way to decrease mileage.

In some cases, community colleges create their own pressures, such as advisory boards that oversee curriculum changes and textbook implementation. In other cases, the pull might be less evident, as in the case of national community college trends such as STEM or credential completion

The concept of *quartering* may bring to mind medieval torture, with our colleges as victims. According to my research, community colleges are far from victims. In fact, all the sites in my study behaved strategically and were able to effectively neutralize many external pressures. Despite the demands of their environments, the sites in my study were able to thrive, solidify their identities, and find different paths to strategic success.

As you can see, I've identified four major categories of external pressure, all pulling the community college at the center. Understanding the impact of these pressures is essential to understanding the entire community college ecosystem. Let's begin.

The Quartering of Community Colleges

Community
- Industry groups
- Advisory boards
- Local governing boards
- Military partners

State Gov't
- Legislators
- Governors
- Political groups

The Community College

Regulators
- Accreditors
- Universities
- State statutes
- Federal regulations/laws

Other CCs
- Sister schools
- National CC trends
- Higher ed trends (STEM)

Community

As many community colleges boast, "Community" is our middle name. Maintaining relationships with local communities is not only essential to our long-term success, but in some cases it is required by state or county statute. Community colleges must be responsive to their local communities by listening to their needs, training the local workforce, and providing quality educational services. Nowhere is this more apparent than at rural community colleges across the United States. These schools are financially supported by their local communities and, more often than not, the dominant provider of higher education in the area.

Along with contributing to the theory of academic capitalism, the University of Arizona's Dr. Gary Rhoades has written extensively about the strategic positioning activities of universities[30] [31]. Dr. Rhoades calls for institutions to be more involved with local communities and take advantage of the unique opportunities afforded by surrounding regions (southwest studies in the southwest, coastal studies in coastal areas, seismic studies near fault lines, etc.).

In addition, Dr. Rhoades suggests that schools should fight the pressure to mirror what other colleges are doing. This trap is easy to fall into when one reads articles or attends a conference session about an exciting idea that worked in another community. Each college should invest in its own distinctive strategic niche. True innovation is defined by uniqueness.

> Each college should invest in its own distinctive strategic niche. True innovation is defined by uniqueness.

I recently attended a presentation detailing the creation of the Community College of Qatar (http://ccq.edu.qa) in 2010. This school (CCQ) was created as a partnership between Houston Community College (HCC) and Qatar's Supreme Education Council. The merger was an attempt to export the U.S. community college model to the oil-rich nation of Qatar and has, by most accounts, been a rousing success. This type of innovation is extremely difficult to replicate because it required enormous resources (both financial and human). This type of initiative certainly wouldn't work for most community colleges, which lack the resources and expertise to build a successful school in a far off country in the Middle East. However, I imagine other colleges will attempt to replicate the HCC/CCQ partnership, not truly understanding the size and scope of the project and the unique synergies that made this partnership a success.

---

30 Rhoades, Gary. "Distinctive choices in intersecting markets: Seeking strategic niches." *Future of the American public research university* (2007): 121-143.

31 Rhoades, Gary. "Who's doing it right? Strategic activity in public research universities." *The Review of Higher Education* 24, no. 1 (2000): 41-66.

The colleges in my study were all impacted (in varying degrees) by community pressures.

Each of them found varying levels of success, but all are actively engaged with their community partners at all possible levels. Grants and Reserves Community College has the highest level of success in managing community pressures. As an embedded community college, GRCC maintains a web of symbiotic relationships. For example, it serves as the official grant evaluator for local K-12 districts, thereby saving those districts thousands of dollars. Additionally, members of GRCC's executive team also serve as volunteer board members for influential community organizations within their service area (private industry council, hospital board, and non-profits). At a time when many community colleges struggled for external funds, GRCC took its case to their constituents through a $60 million bond measure that passed with over 60 percent of the vote.

> As leaders, we should never enter a relationship with the sole purpose of seeking revenue. I encourage you to find relationships that are mutually beneficial and based on shared objectives.

As leaders, we should never enter a relationship with the sole purpose of seeking revenue. I encourage you to find relationships that are mutually beneficial and based on shared objectives. If those relationships do result in financial support, then let that support be a fortunate by-product of your efforts to create enduring and mutually beneficial strategic partnerships.

Private industry advocacy groups such as chambers of commerce or private industry councils may exert pressure on community colleges to keep property taxes as low as possible, and align scholastic programs to meet their specific industry needs. This is especially true in areas where private industry plays a prominent role in the local economy through manufacturing, the energy sector, the defense industry, tourism, and other activities. In an attempt to meet their specific needs for workers, industry leaders often try to influence curriculum and can steer programs away from our traditional core competencies.

A provost at one of my sites shared the details of an initiative he oversaw in another state, involving a manufacturing and heavy equipment operator program. These programs are expensive when schools need to purchase high dollar vehicles and equipment, plus maintain and house the programs. The provost arranged a partnership with John Deere whereby they provided machines at no cost to the institution, in exchange for offering the programs.

Ultimately, students benefit the most from symbiotic partnerships like the one with John Deere. They gain access to sophisticated equipment and valuable hands-on training while the institution saves millions of dollars. Managing these pressures can prove challenging and perhaps frustrating at times, but truly innovative partnerships can emerge.

Local advisory boards can exert pressure at the discipline/ program level to align curriculum with their specific needs. Crystal Ball Community College (CBCC) feels pressure from local power plants in this way. Bridge and Buffer Community College (BBCC) feels pressure from its local military installation and supporting industries.

> A delicate balance exists between advisory boards and the community colleges they advise.

Grants and Reserves Community College (GRCC) feels pressure from local law enforcement organizations. A delicate balance exists between advisory boards and the community colleges they advise. As a department chair, I've managed many advisory board meetings, and I always make sure I'm clear about the objectives and expectations of each meeting. I let everyone know that we, as faculty, are there to listen. Our goal is to listen more than we speak. I also make it clear that we will organize their feedback, evaluate their needs, and take action.

Each group appreciates the fact that I always complete the loop. For example, our most recent advisory board meeting resulted in a new cyber security degree at Cochise College. The process took six months, but I was able to show the advisory group that we did indeed use their feedback to create this new credential. I typically ask our advisory boards to list the skills they'd like to see our students (their future employees) possess at graduation. Our role as faculty is to then translate those skills into specific courses, which in turn will lead to more valuable degrees and better employment opportunities for our students.

Each community college in my study feels the pressure of being governed by a locally-elected board that represents different parts of their service areas. Schools that serve a geographically-dispersed service area have a strategic disadvantage. Maintaining centers and outreach facilities in multiple cities, many of which serve sparsely-populated communities, is highly inefficient for at least two of the sites. Consider that all are rural community colleges. Some sites feel pressure to invest in remote communities within their service area to garner the support of governing board members who represent those areas. Some respond to this pressure by maintaining multiple remote facilities that often require redundant employees, such as advisors and support staff. This is just one of the community pressures faced by many colleges.

As I have shown, community pressures can be turned into strategic advantages through the coordinated and concerted effort to turn your institution into an *embedded community college*; an institution deeply rooted in its community through a variety of relationships with local community partners.

State Government

The most significant pressures associated with state government in this study are financial. The sites in my study receive anywhere from 10 to 30 percent of their annual budgets from the state government.

Some community colleges in the state have purposefully allowed the state-funded portion of their budget to dip below 10 percent to minimize the pressure on their institution. Based the adage, "If you don't expect anything, you won't be disappointed," developing alternative funding sources helps prevent panic when the state legislature makes further cuts.

It appears as though Grants and Reserves Community College is headed in this direction. They secured large amounts of funding through grants and local bond initiatives and have reached a point where they not only replaced lost state allocations, but have exceeded the amount of lost funding.

Each state has its own labyrinth of funding issues for community colleges, including political groups that wield influence with state legislators.

Each state has its own labyrinth of funding issues for community colleges, including political groups that wield influence with state legislators. Often, tax-related proposals need the support of these groups before reaching state legislators. As a researcher, I found this fascinating. This particular state has a politically-connected lobbying entity with the power to kill any tax-related proposal before it even gets to a committee. The organization helped pass a law that limits the amount a community college can raise property taxes each year. All three sites in my study know this lobbying organization by name and recognize the influence it wields with legislators and the governor's office. Both BBCC and CBCC employ their own professional lobbyist to work with legislators and the governor's office in hopes of neutralizing these types of negative pressures.

Regulators

The sites in my study suffer from a never-ending barrage of regulatory pressures. My findings suggest this type of quartering pressure is the most restrictive and difficult of all pressures. In many cases, statutory restrictions prevent community colleges from using ideal solutions to neutralize specific problems. In other cases, colleges must expend huge amounts of energy and resources to comply with changing federal regulations or state reporting requirements.

Regulators require compliance. The consequence of non-compliance may include censorship by accrediting bodies, reduced funding, or restrictions placed on a school's ability to offer federal financial aid. Each of these outcomes is strategically catastrophic. For example, changes to federal financial aid requirements had a large impact on enrollment at Bridge and Buffer Community College. The Vice President for Instruction reported that approximately 30 percent fewer students received federal financial aid than the previous year because of new regulations. Other schools reported the need to hire additional personnel or assign extra duties to existing personnel to comply with regulations. While Crystal Ball Community College has opted out of the federal student loan program, opting out of the Pell grant system would prove strategically disastrous because it would disadvantage so many of its students.

Universities are also in the regulators category based on their ability to apply curricular pressure and their leading role in discipline-specific accreditation. Earlier in this chapter I discussed the silo effect—the loyalty of faculty to their disciplines and the potentially detrimental nature of this narrow view. (This is in reference to the influential book written by Christopher Jencks and David Riesman in 1968 titled *The Academic Revolution*.)[32]

---

[32] Jencks, Christopher, and David Riesman. "The academic revolution." (1968).

Discipline loyalty was on display at each college in my study. For example, much of what is offered in the field of chemistry is dictated by the American Chemical Society, a professional organization of chemists. Courses in health-related fields, such as nursing, are standardized by accrediting bodies and statewide boards of nursing. Who influences these associations? Many are driven by university professors who exert a significant influence on community colleges by promoting a specific curriculum to professional associations and accrediting bodies.

Also, universities govern the course transfer process. In the case of BBCC, 26 percent of their students transfer to a university. In order to meet the needs of those students, BBCC is required to modify its curriculum to meet the direction of its university partners.

State statutory limitations create the most restrictive of all pressures in the regulators category. The colleges in my study were severely limited in two specific areas: annual budget and property taxes. In this particular state, statutes limit the total amount of a community college's annual budget based on a formula that considers population, inflation, and the institution's budget 30 years ago. Leaders at CBCC are currently trying to manage this crisis. The situation is that they are fiscally healthy with considerable financial reserves, yet budget limitation statutes prevent them from spending beyond a set amount.

Community colleges in this state are also limited in raising property taxes, which can only go up by a certain percent each year. This inhibits one of their three major revenue streams.

To summarize: We see this state (and many other states) reducing funds to community colleges. Adding insult to injury, state laws and regulations limit each institution's ability to increase one of their primary revenue streams. Other statutes prevent colleges from spending reserves they may have built-up through prudent financial planning if their budgets exceed the limit dictated by the state's budget limitation statute.

Other Community Colleges

The pressures exerted by other community colleges may be the most difficult to recognize or to measure. These pressures may not be as tangible as a state statute, a memo from a governing board member, or the new federal financial aid regulations, but they do impact the sites in my study. Colleges affect one another in both positive and negative ways.

The community colleges in my study were part of a complex dynamic formed by state reductions and statewide associations for community colleges, leading to different strategies for dealing with issues. Each school was affected by national trends, beyond their local issues. This included the voluntary accountability framework promoted by the American Association of Community Colleges; the trend to fund STEM-related activities; and the trend toward measuring completion, to name a few.

For example, at BBCC, the pressure to increase the number of degree completers led the school to implement policies that favor students who have declared a major and are actively seeking a degree. As a department chair at BBCC shared with me, this seems to be having a negative effect on "lifelong learner" students who wish to simply take one or two classes in hopes of acquiring specific skills, such as welding, carpentry, and automotive. These students are pressured to declare a major or lose access to support services and financial aid. This is just one example of pressure from within the community college system.

When we recognize the potential for positive growth from negative pressure, institutions can use adversity to their strategic advantage.

Now we've looked at multiple pressures that pull community colleges in four directions at once. While the Quartering concept connotes torture, each of these external pressures can be converted from negative to positive energy by building strong relationships and seeking community partnerships. When we recognize the potential for positive growth from negative pressure, institutions can use adversity to their strategic advantage. This is part of what I present in the following section and in more detail in Chapters Five and Six.

Possessing a Mandate to Neutralize Pressures

In the previous section, I introduced a new framework to analyze the pressures community colleges face. Dividing these influences into four quadrants makes it easier to identify and deal with each category

In this section, I propose another new approach related to those quartering pressures: a **mandate to neutralize**. This approach can best be described as a determined, deliberate, and coordinated approach to neutralize forces that exert pressure on an institution.

Each of the colleges in my study used a variety of neutralizing activities, with varying success. The leaders of GRCC focused on neutralizing pressure from regulators and local communities, whereas CBCC concentrated on neutralizing issues with state government and other community colleges through statewide associations.

A mandate to neutralize can best be described as a determined, deliberate, and coordinated approach to neutralize forces that exert pressure on an institution.

Of all the sites in this study, BBCC came closest to achieving a clear mandate to neutralize. However, while BBCC used aggressive neutralizing activities for each of the four quartering categories (community, state government, regulators, and other community colleges), the college did not use a formal, coordinated approach, and also lacked a mechanism to track the results its efforts. Despite that, the upper administration at BBCC seemed to possess an elevated understanding of the importance of neutralizing external pressures, and they participated in a variety of activities designed to protect the institution from these potentially negative influences.

> My research shows that institutions with a clear mandate to neutralize external pressures are able to increase their capacity for strategic behavior.

Dr. Martin Meznar and Dr. Douglas Nigh authored an article in the *Academy of Management Journal*[33] in 1995 in which they discuss managing external pressures on institutions. They labeled activities designed to protect institutions as *buffering* activities. They identified activities designed to conform or comply with external pressures as *bridging* activities. At BBCC, these bridging activities are on display at different levels of the college, but most notably in the middle, where administrators and staff work to meet frequently changing requirements of federal financial aid, the latest reauthorization of the Higher Education Act, and the cyclical requirements of its regional accrediting body.

My research shows that institutions with a clear mandate to neutralize external pressures are able to increase their capacity for strategic behavior. Once these pressures are identified and neutralized (through bridging and buffering), community colleges are free to strategize, innovate, and satisfy the needs of their local communities.

The most successful colleges understood that the mandate to neutralize might involve not only neutralizing external pressures, but perhaps turning those detriments into positive, mutually-beneficial relationships.

---

33 Meznar, Martin B., and Douglas Nigh. "Buffer or bridge? Environmental and organizational determinants of public affairs activities in American firms." *Academy of Management Journal* 38, no. 4 (1995): 975-996.

The Isomorphic Huddle

In Chapter Two, I introduced the three traditional forms of isomorphism (coercive, mimetic, and normative). It seems community colleges behave similarly and copy one another in an effort to legitimize themselves to state and local government (coercive isomorphism). They behave similarly due to uncertainty (mimetic isomorphism), while also increasing their collaborative efforts through statewide associations (normative isomorphism).

> Just as a football team huddles to plan the next play, these community colleges responded by banding together to plan their next move.

For community colleges, the lines between the different forms of isomorphism are less distinct than with other types of institutions. In response to drastic state funding cuts, members of the upper administration at all colleges in my study formed what can best be called an **isomorphic huddle**. Just as a football team huddles to plan the next play, these community colleges responded by banding together to plan their next move. They were more involved with statewide community college professional associations. The statewide association of community college presidents became more active, as did the statewide group for chief financial officers. Groups that met sporadically with casual agendas, now participated in intense isomorphic huddling. They hoped to strategize, and eventually strengthen the strategic position of community colleges in the state. This was an attempt to prevent further cuts or some other equally damaging state-level decision.

The Ecosystem

As you consider your current role, and perhaps the community college leadership role you aspire to, I encourage you to use the tools in this chapter to broaden your perspective. Consider the term *ecosystem*: a community of dynamic entities interacting to maintain a complex system that thrives on their interactions and energies.

Community colleges now face difficult decisions, given the reality of reduced financial resources. This fiscal climate is forcing community colleges to re-prioritize, re-allocate, and look closely at their strategic position in higher education. Shall we crumble? Never. We are resilient. We thrive on adversity, in part because we understand the ecosystem in which we exist. We partner. We comply. We strategize. We innovate. And we rarely fail.

Your job as an innovative leader is to learn as much as you can about the forces that exert pressure on community colleges.

This fiscal climate is forcing community colleges to re-prioritize, re-allocate, and look closely at their strategic position in higher education.

Manage those pressures. Bridge, buffer, or both. You may find that your influence will nudge your institution in truly innovative strategic directions.

Chapter 5

Community College Strategy

*O*ne of my favorite lectures during each semester is when I introduce case studies showing how specific companies use technology to create competitive strategic advantages. Walmart is easily the crown jewel of case studies in this regard. In 1987, they launched a satellite into space for a reported $24 million. This satellite would serve as the hub to link all Walmart stores, distribution centers, and suppliers in hopes of automating their inventory worldwide. Like many great ideas, the premise of this one was simple: Walmart would always have what you came to buy. If you came to Walmart to buy a Snickers bar, then Walmart would have that Snickers bar. If you came to Walmart for 2 percent milk, then Walmart would always have 2 percent milk. Walmart's inventory of every item would never be depleted.

Implementing this grand design was a complicated feat, involving the launch of a historic satellite, developing custom software, and distributing hardware to support this enormous project. Now, when a cashier at Walmart scans an item for purchase, that item is automatically deducted from inventory.

When the inventory for that particular item decreases to a predetermined threshold, an order is automatically (with no human intervention) submitted to the supplier, who in turn fills the order and initiates transport of that product to the nearest distribution center or store. During the 1990s and into the early 2000s, all Walmart locations had a satellite dish on their rooftops to communicate with Walmart's satellite. Thanks to the exponential increase of Internet bandwidth, you'd be hard-pressed to find a satellite dish on any Walmart store rooftop today. I often joke in class that I wish my car operated this way when my low fuel indicator comes on. If so, Chevron would automatically send a fuel truck with gasoline when I need it.

In 1990, Walmart's 1,550 stores accounted for $25 billion in revenue. Today, Walmart has over 11,000 locations with an annual revenue of $475 billion. Their electronic data interchange network and inventory control system remains one of the most strategically successful innovations in the history of private enterprise. They demonstrated incredible foresight, light years ahead of the competition. Walmart's leadership saw the potential for technology to drive growth and profitability for decades into the future, leading to a huge competitive advantage in the marketplace.

What can community colleges learn from Walmart? What new ideas might help us shape the strategic direction of our schools?

Around the time Walmart launched their satellite, K-mart was the largest discount retailer in the world. Since then, Walmart has experienced tremendous growth, while K-mart's annual revenue is approximately half of what it was in 1990.

I often challenge my class to envision what "technology" meant in 1987. Familiarity with brick cell phones, the Commodore 64, or playing Oregon Trail on the Apple IIe would have qualified you as a techie back then. Walmart was so far ahead of its time that much of the technology to support their electronic data interchange network did not yet exist.

What can community colleges learn from Walmart? What new ideas might help us shape the strategic direction of our schools? How can we create positive changes that will set our institutions apart? What can we learn from the innovative practices of private industry?

Your Ability to Lead

In this section, I'd like you to think about what defines you as a leader. What do you stand for? What are you passionate about, and how do you communicate that passion to the people around you? Are you the type of college leader who inspires faculty and staff? Are you well-respected at your institution? Do others seek your counsel?

Leadership at a community college can come from all levels of the institution.

As you consider these questions, I want you to understand that leadership at a community college can come from all levels of the institution. My research shows many examples of strategic activities, in a variety of forms, regardless of job title.

I want you to think about the *great* leaders you've known. What made them outstanding? Why did people follow them? What do these leaders have in common? When I think of all the great leaders who have influenced me, they all share two common traits. First, they are excellent communicators. Communication comes naturally to some people, while others must work to develop these skills. No matter how they acquire their skills, charismatic leaders communicate a clear vision. They understand that in order to garner followers, they must convince people they stand for something important.

Second, these great leaders also provided me with the *tools* to be successful.

From 2007 to 2010, I served as the Assistant Dean of Technology at Cochise College. In my plan for the division, which included industrial technology (welding, construction, automotive, agriculture, business, and computer information systems), community relationships were a high priority. I spotted opportunities for our division to help community organizations (nonprofits, schools, social service agencies) through projects that would give our students valuable hands-on learning. I met with representatives from different groups, and each gave me a list of three to five potential projects. These projects included servicing a fleet of vehicles for a social services agency, technology presentations to local elementary schools, multiple construction projects for area nonprofits, and more.

> As a leader, you know you've succeeded when you craft a vision, communicate that vision, provide the tools to reach that vision, and finally, see faculty and staff adopt your vision as their own.

At our kickoff meeting to start the academic year, I first introduced my community relationship vision for the division and explained how we could have an enormous strategic impact on our surrounding communities. I then presented the list of specific projects for "adoption." To my delight, many of those projects were immediately adopted.

As a leader, you know you've succeeded when you craft a vision, communicate that vision, provide the tools to reach that vision, and finally, see faculty and staff adopt your vision as their own.

The final important piece of this story came at the end of this academic year, when many of these projects were successfully completed by the faculty and students who adopted them. I formally recognized the responsible faculty with community involvement awards signed by myself, the Vice President of Instruction, and the President of Cochise College. I knew it was important to recognize everyone who helped make my vision a reality. To this day, these faculty members proudly and prominently display the awards in their offices.

Embedded Community Colleges

Strategic positioning is the collective (not necessarily coordinated) effort of stakeholders to shape and define the priorities, objectives, and direction of a particular institution. Strategically successful institutions serve their communities by investing in activities that meet each area's unique needs.

The findings of my study suggest that the term "strategic position" may not be the best way to describe the role of modern community colleges. The word *position* implies a fixed state; a clear and obvious place nestled between K-12 and university partners. My findings suggest the role of the modern community college is more fluid. Our schools are agile entities instead of stodgy institutions; more adaptive than traditional. Modern community colleges are moving targets, constantly adapting and reacting to external pressures.

> Our schools are agile entities instead of stodgy institutions; more adaptive than traditional. Modern community colleges are moving targets, constantly adapting and reacting to external pressures.

The strategic orientation of community colleges has clearly changed. My research shows that schools have pivoted away from relying on state allocations and moved closer to their local communities for financial support. Students have to bear more of the burden through slow and steady tuition increases. Local taxpayers are asked to bear more of the burden through a slow, steady increase in property taxes. Colleges are bearing more of the financial burden through budget cuts, reductions to their workforces, and constrained financial stewardship practices.

As state support dwindles and more institutions pivot to their new, community-focused *strategic orientation*, deeply *embedded community colleges* will enjoy the strongest, most enduring strategic positions.

Embedded Community Colleges

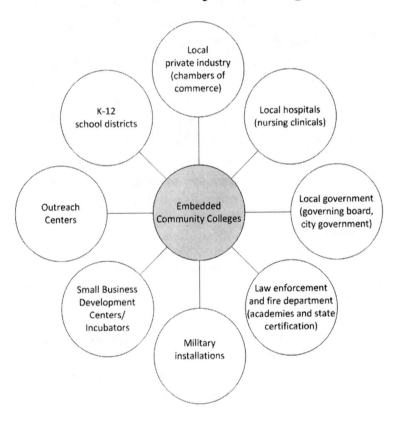

Embedded community colleges place a high priority on establishing and maintaining relationships with members of their local communities. Local community networks are an important part of being embedded. Community colleges partner with local military installations, engage in nursing clinical partnerships with local hospitals, partner with local K-12 school districts in hopes of attracting their graduates, and respond to the needs of local industry representatives. Embedded schools also encourage college leaders to serve on the boards of community organizations and partners. These colleges often assist local towns and cities with their economic development, partner with local law enforcement and fire departments to train future professionals in those areas, stimulate entrepreneurial activity through small business development centers, and learn to understand and appreciate the nuances of local politics.

In any of the communities served by the schools in my study, I needed only refer to "the college," and community members knew exactly what I meant. In almost all cases, the community college is the dominant provider of higher education services in the area. While universities may have a presence, they aren't "The College." Embedded community colleges are respected and revered in their areas, and as these institutions become more reliant on local communities, they will enjoy the strongest possible strategic positions.

Embedded Activities

As I examined the impact of reduced financial resources on the strategic positioning activities of community colleges, I found that drastic state reductions forced many schools to act quickly. Some of those responses were strategic, while others were more reactionary.

The most successful responses were the *quartering of community colleges* approach coupled with a *mandate to neutralize*. These approaches don't guarantee strategic success, but they do enhance a college's ability to create meaningful changes. Strategically successful community colleges seize new opportunities by pivoting away from state government and becoming more focused than ever on the needs of the populations they serve.

This new strategic orientation brings pressures of its own. Meeting the needs of diverse and widely scattered communities may lead to inefficiency, but these colleges seem to understand that some inefficiency is necessary to garner support from stakeholders across their entire service area. For example, CBCC maintains multiple centers in far-off regions of its service area that require considerable investment for a relatively small group of students.

Let's take a look at specific examples of community colleges behaving strategically to support their goal of becoming embedded community colleges.

Example 1: Buffering and Neutralizing by Upper Administration

Members of the upper administration at Bridge and Buffer Community College are heavily involved in bridging and buffering external pressures by using two strategies. First, BBCC employs a legislative lobbyist who represents its interests at the state government level. Second, all members of BBCC's upper administration are now active in statewide professional associations in an attempt to prevent future harmful events, such as the recent 50 percent state allocation reduction to community colleges.

Effective Lobbying Activities

Bridge and Buffer Community College and Crystal Ball Community College share the same lobbyist. She is extremely effective in representing their interests at the state government level through various activities. The President of CBCC refers to her as a "weapon." According to both presidents (BBCC and CBCC), she lets them know about potentially harmful decisions early in the process. This advanced warning gives them time to plan and implement strategies in hopes of producing the best possible outcome for their institutions.

One of the most significant strategic findings of my study involves the role of this lobbyist in securing a new revenue stream from the state, which the President of CBCC described as "sleight of hand."

The two presidents and their lobbyist strategized that since the nationwide trend was toward science, technology, engineering, and math, it might make sense to push for a STEM-related revenue stream. Legislators would be able to tout their support for STEM while demonstrating their support for community colleges. Both CBCC and BBCC made the proactive, strategic decision to approach the state in hopes of generating a new revenue stream from the same entity that slashed its allocation to community colleges by 50 percent. Ultimately, their efforts were successful and all community colleges in the state now benefit from this new stream of revenue.

Increased Activity of Statewide Associations

Leaders from nearly all community colleges in this state are more actively involved in statewide professional groups, hoping to provide a unified force against future adverse actions. In Chapter Four, I labeled this phenomenon the **isomorphic huddle**. So far, these statewide groups have been effective. Community colleges in this state can present a united front overall, and also through each of these groups. When further cuts or other adverse actions are proposed by state government, community colleges now present a strong, united defense.

The professional groups not only help protect community colleges, but also initiate proactive campaigns to improve conditions. For example, the statewide CFO association actively lobbied the state legislature in hopes of modifying the statute governing revenue bonds. These bonds allow institutions to borrow money while pledging future revenue, often in the form of tuition. The former statute allowed institutions to allot just 25 percent of the total revenue bond to instruction-related activities. Based largely on the legislative lobbying efforts of BBCC's chief financial officer, the revenue bond statute was changed and now allows for 100 percent of the bond to be used for instruction. This means that when community colleges issue $10 million in revenue bonds, all $10 million can now be used to build and equip classrooms.

Example 2: Identification and Clear Communication of Strategic Concepts

At Bridge and Buffer Community College, members of the upper administration direct strategic activity. Once strategic concepts and priorities are identified from the top, funding and resources flow outward in concentric circles. Burton Clark's concept of a core[34] of activities that steer an institution is on display at BBCC. Instruction is clearly the core function of BBCC, and certain disciplines (Nursing, Aviation, Technology, and the thriving Online Campus) are identified as strategic strengths. These areas receive extra resources and freedom because of their distinction.

In terms of concentric circle funding, the upper administration clearly defines the strategic strengths, and then unapologetically allocates resources to support those areas. This may seem controversial and even unfair, but I see it differently. I see it as transparent leadership. The administration clearly identified areas with competitive advantages. While faculty and staff at other institutions might have to guess why their administration gives extra resources to the welding department year after year, BBCC's administration clearly communicates

---

34 Clark, Burton R. *Creating Entrepreneurial Universities: Organizational Pathways of Transformation. Issues in Higher Education.* Elsevier Science Regional Sales, 665 Avenue of the Americas, New York, NY 10010 (paperback: ISBN-0-08-0433545; hardcover: ISBN-0-08-0433421)., 1998.

that certain programs are considered strategic strengths and receive more resources than other areas.

BBCC clearly defined its strategic priorities and concepts, and then tied these concepts to the budgeting process. Organizations with high priority are given a certain degree of autonomy in their operations, allowing them to experiment with different strategic initiatives without fear of losing funds or being censored.

In addition to funding these strategic strengths, BBCC identifies a set of guiding strategic principles, specifically: employee-friendly, future-focused, and student-centered. They clearly communicate these principles at college-wide events and through other formal communications. At BBCC, employees understand that all decisions made by the upper administration will be connected in some way to these three principles. This transparency creates a high level of trust between upper administration and BBCC's employees.

BBCC clearly defined its strategic priorities and concepts, and then tied these concepts to the budgeting process. Organizations with high priority are given a certain degree of autonomy in their operations, allowing them to experiment with different strategic initiatives without fear of losing funds or being censored.

Example 3: Strategic Flexibility

Leaders at BBCC understand the community college ecosystem is one of shifting concepts and changing priorities (local, state, and national) with paradigms that cycle through the ecosystem. A few years ago the focus was on managing enrollment. Now the focus seems to be on completion and accountability. Before that, it was access and success in higher education. Understanding the nature of the ever changing, dynamic community college ecosystem allows BBCC leaders to adapt quickly and easily.

Leaders at both BBCC and GRCC espouse the concept of strategic flexibility and how it allows leaders to embrace opportunities that arise. The following examples from my study demonstrate this. Coincidentally, both involve solar power.

Serendipitous Strategic Initiatives

Up to this point, the concept of embedded community colleges has focused on colleges in active pursuit of partnerships with their many stakeholders. Sometimes colleges benefit by responding to unexpected opportunities from our stakeholders. Each of our stakeholders is motivated by their own set of goals and objectives which may or may not overlap with ours. As we actively seek partnerships, we should be willing to listen, observe, survey the landscape, and be open to new ideas. Sometimes these new propositions give our students valuable learning opportunities, allow our faculty to grow professionally, and make our institution part of innovative activities with our local partners.

> Sometimes colleges benefit by responding to unexpected opportunities from our stakeholders.

If you drove past the smaller of Bridge and Buffer Community College's two main campuses, you would see an impressive field of parabolic solar arrays that span the size of a football field. These arrays track the sun as it passes across the sky to maximize the amount of energy gathered. The energy gathered is then used to both heat and cool various facilities at BBCC, saving tens of thousands of dollars annually and reducing the institution's reliance on non-renewable energy.

According to a member of BBCC's upper administration, this project "just fell into our laps when the power company approached us out of nowhere." As an innovative and strategic leader, if you're able to recognize opportunities like this, you'll become involved in activities that have a profound impact on your institution. Despite the fact that you're constantly pushed and pulled in different directions, grand opportunities will show up now and then. Perhaps it will come as voicemail message from a former student about a chance to be involved in the next DARPA grand challenge. Or it might be an email from the CEO of the local power company wanting to discuss a new venture. You might open an email from a military commander asking if your school would like to be involved in unmanned aerial vehicle training. If you're able to recognize and capitalize on these unique opportunities, you will quickly establish yourself as an innovative and respected leader.

As you enter the main campus for Grants and Reserves Community College, the solar arrays are hard to miss. A handful of different types of arrays are on display across campus—on rooftops, stretched across fields, adorning the entrance, and more. Many people in the community have referred to the arrays an architectural masterpiece.

Despite the fact that you're constantly pushed and pulled in different directions, grand opportunities will show up now and then.

The president of GRCC estimates they save approximately $1 million each year from the five megawatt arrays (enough to power approximately 500 homes). The project came about when a private company approached GRCC in hopes of partnering with them. The college ended up paying absolutely nothing for the arrays, yet is still able to reap the benefit of energy cost savings. Recently, GRCC entered discussions to create entrepreneurial incubator sites using the solar arrays. The school will also use this project in their new engineering program partnership with the local state university.

Example 4: Strategic Significance of Financial Reserves

As previously mentioned, my research indicates community colleges are placing more financial burdens on local communities through increased property taxes, and on their students through increased tuition and fees. Additionally, all three sites in my study have initiated aggressive financial reserve initiatives.

Financial reserves allowed Bridge and Buffer Community College to weather the storm of reduced state allocations and invest in resource-intensive strategic priorities, including new facilities, renovations, and funding areas near the core of the institution. Without these reserves, state budget cuts would have hit BBCC much harder.

According to BBCC's president, the school responded to state reductions by reducing resources in certain areas, reductions in force through attrition, and "cutting the fat." One might expect an organization that receives 30 percent of its revenue from that state to react more severely or exhibit some signs of crisis. But BBCC refused to let budget cuts affect the core of the institution—instructional activities.

I examined BBCC's annual financial statements and discovered that over the past ten years, BBCC allocated significant sums of money to reserve accounts, ostensibly to be used for weathering the type of reductions it experienced in FY2012 (drastic state allocation reduction). The reserves for the current budget year alone totaled 50 percent of BBCC's overall budget and have been as high as 60 percent of its overall budget over the past ten years. While these funds were initially set aside to fund future capital projects, they were used to replace some of the state allocation reductions, thereby lessening the impact of those reductions on BBCC. This strategy was years in the making and required extraordinary foresight. Ultimately, it allowed BBCC to weather adverse financial conditions.

Grants and Reserves Community College also implemented an aggressive financial reserve strategy, with reserve accounts totaling close to an entire year's budget. The strategic asset of these reserves not only helped neutralize drastic state budget cuts, but also allowed the school to invest in strategic initiatives.

The president of GRCC told me he and the administration have purposefully and consistently spent only 92-93 percent of their annual budget; holding back the remaining 7-8 percent in an unrestricted fund reserve account that grew over the years, at times in excess of an entire year's budget.

Focusing on alternative streams of revenue and accumulating sizable financial reserves allowed GRCC to decrease its reliance on state support, which at this point accounts for only 10 percent of GRCC's annual budget. By reducing its reliance on state government and increasing its reliance on reserves and local community partners, GRCC is committed to a new, community-focused, embedded community college strategic orientation as a long-term strategy.

Crystal Ball Community College maintains a reserve account balance equal to approximately half a year's budget. This reserve account has actually been larger than an entire year's budget in the past. As with other community colleges, the practice of maintaining large financial reserves has allowed it to engage in strategic activity and neutralize the impact of drastic state funding reductions; the most significant example being the construction of a new $5 million career technical education center funded exclusively by CBCC's reserves.

According to the CFO of CBCC, accumulating cash reserves is also an attempt to protect the college against future reductions or future decline in property valuation. If CBCC does encounter adverse financial conditions, the reserves should give them enough time to manage the crisis.

Example 5: Grants as Strategic Supplemental Assets

The sheer amount of grant funding received by Grants and Reserves Community College is staggering; approximately

60 percent of its total annual budget in a recent fiscal year. Grant funding, along with its financial reserves, helped GRCC neutralize part of the negative impact from state budget cuts. While reserves offer GRCC complete freedom to spend without regulatory or external involvement, grants are tied to specific initiatives, most of which align with the institution's strategic strengths. Other grants are designed to increase activity in areas outside the traditional core of activities at GRCC. In this way, grants have the potential to either *supplement* an institution's strategic positioning efforts or *supplant* the institution's strategic positioning efforts.

Grants allowed the school to undertake initiatives that wouldn't have been possible otherwise. Clearly, these grants also affected the GRCC's strategic positioning as the college pivoted to align itself with requirements for each respective grant, such as a focus on engineering, an emphasis on STEM, or career technical education.

> While it may be tempting to go after certain multi-million dollar grants, they may be more trouble than they're worth and not serve the college's strategic interests. Grants should always *supplement* and never *supplant* our strategic goals.

During austere times, community college leaders logically seek alternative revenue (grants) to replace lost revenue streams (state allocations). However, the pursuit and acceptance of grant funding should align with the school's strategic objectives. Leaders must understand that accepting grant funding outside areas of core competence will require additional internal investment and expertise. These costs should be considered when pursuing all types of grant funds. While it may be tempting to go after certain multi-million dollar grants, they may be more trouble than they're worth and not serve the college's strategic interests. Grants should always *supplement* and never *supplant* **our** strategic goals.

Example 6: Embedded Community Colleges are Supported Community Colleges

Grants and Reserves Community College is deeply embedded in its local community through a variety of relationships and partnerships. In many ways, GRCC is a pillar in its community as the dominant provider of higher education services. This college has essentially commoditized local community support through local bond initiatives to the tune of $60 million.

Multiple leaders at GRCC shared with me the high level of importance placed on being "good neighbors" in the community and respecting the role they play as a *community* college. A few years ago, GRCC convened a community task force with the goal of initiating a $10 million local bond campaign. Due in large part to the strong and respected strategic role of GRCC in the community, this task force recommended the total amount of the bond be increased to $60 million. The leadership at GRCC reluctantly agreed to the amount and were pleasantly surprised when the $60 million bond initiative passed with over 60 percent of voter support.

Partnerships have been a part of GRCC's identity for many years. In fact, GRCC's mission statement references innovative partnerships and this concept is ingrained in leaders at all levels of the school. Over the years, GRCC has formed partnerships with a wide variety of organizations, including the local hospital, the industry council, a local military installation, local industry representatives, the K-12 district, and a long-standing relationship with one of the state's universities that has a branch campus on the main campus of GRCC. These partnerships account for GRCC's embedded status.

GRCC's president shared a fascinating story about its role as an embedded community college. Each year, the administration and governing board have the ability to raise property taxes on the local residential and commercial population. One particular year, similar to other years, the administration recommended a

2 percent property tax increase. At a meeting, the president of the local chamber of commerce stated this 2 percent increase would be an extreme hardship on area businesses who were still suffering through the great recession and struggling to recover. The upper administration called for a recess, met privately, then returned to the board meeting and reversed their recommendation—essentially leaving $500,000 on the table. The upper administration realized the importance of being a good neighbor and listened to the needs of local businesses. Decisions like this one give GRCC an esteemed position in the area. Their decision to leave $500,000 on the table most certainly helped pass the $60 million bond measure that allowed the school to do so much more.

Example 7: Active Ecosystem Awareness and Foresight

Crystal Ball Community College is acutely aware of its environment and the intricacies of the community college ecosystem (see Chapter 4). Through the lobbying efforts of its president and their contracted lobbyist, plus a commitment to gather information about potential threats from state government, CBCC possesses a *strategic crystal ball.* This crystal ball gave them the foresight to learn of state budget cuts before any other institution in the state, allowing it to respond swiftly and strategically to those cuts.

The administration of CBCC seems keenly aware of the school's external environment. During my conversations with upper administrators and other leaders, each person spoke about the impact of external pressure from CBCC's regional accrediting body, state government, the federal government, private industry, universities, and more. While each of entities brings specific pressure to bear on CBCC, the administration has taken the time to strategize and analyze their institution's relationship with each of these bodies.

The foresight gained through active environmental awareness allowed CBCC to mitigate drastic state cuts through a deliberate and prudent approach versus the more reactive, haphazard approach of an institution without such foresight. Upon learning of the impending state reductions, CBCC responded swiftly by making drastic internal cuts of its own.

The most significant finding at Crystal Ball Community College relates to how leaders anticipated the state's drastic 50 percent reduction in allocations. While other community colleges were caught off guard, CBCC foresaw the cuts one to two years before they actually happened. This allowed CBCC to proactively and strategically mitigate those reductions. The college was actively engaged through the efforts of its contracted lobbyist, the lobbying efforts of its president, and a general commitment from CBCC's upper administration to actively listen to information coming from state government. As a result, CBCC was able to respond in a strategic and planned way when their state budget was reduced. The CFO shared that upper administration always aims to respond to crisis situations in careful and reasonable ways. CBCC immediately closed some of its facilities and significantly reduced the size of administration by approximately $1 million (three vice presidents reduced to two, six deans cut to three, and five divisions reduced to three).

In the above section, we clearly see an institution that responded swiftly, proactively, and strategically to the foresight it gained through a strategy of active environmental awareness.

Example 8: Shared Governance is the Spoonful of Sugar

As we learned in the previous section, Crystal Ball Community College responded to state cuts by swiftly making administrative reductions. Their response also called for a 2 percent reduction in pay for all employees. Clearly, these are difficult decisions to implement at any institution, but it appears they were largely accepted and supported by CBCC's faculty and staff. I connect this directly to the value placed by CBCC's president on the concept of **shared governance** policies and procedures throughout the school.

Implementing shared governance can be a cumbersome logistical challenge. While this has certainly been the case at CBCC, now it is embedded in the culture and garners much support for the administration across CBCC's geographically dispersed locations. Shared governance has been the **spoonful of sugar** that makes the medicine (difficult, typically unpopular decisions) go down.

Shared governance policies and procedures play an important role at CBCC. This is nothing new to higher education. Shared governance is designed to involve and value the input of a multitude of stakeholders. The president of CBCC implemented shared governance through several initiatives that sought input from faculty and staff across the school's large geographic area. This firm and ongoing commitment to shared governance led to positive support from faculty and staff for the difficult financially-driven decisions made by upper administration. Shared governance opened lines of communication, letting the people at CBCC feel actively involved in the college's strategic direction. This kind of active involvement makes tough decisions easier to swallow.

Although no one in upper administration mentioned the impact of shared governance during difficult times, I believe this school-wide policy greatly increased support for the administration's sensitive and challenging decisions in response to state funding cuts.

Example 9: Predictive Program Development

Crystal Ball Community College serves two of the most economically depressed counties in the state and perhaps across the nation (depending on the metrics used). Private industry is largely non-existent and all other sectors of the economy have been severely impacted by the great recession.

Rather than simply waiting to see what other industries might develop in its county, CBCC has taken a **predictive** strategic direction. This means they attempt to predict what industries will materialize in the county and begin investing in academic programs to support those potential new jobs. For example, CBCC invested time and money to develop a new applied engineering program. In addition, they added instructional activities related to mining and forestry operations.

Time will tell regarding the success of this investment and direction. The predictive approach comes with considerable risk should these industries fail to materialize. In some cases, CBCC draws from financial reserves and grants to fund these efforts, which allows them to minimize the risk.

Conclusion

In ancient Greece, the title and position of *strategos* was given to select military leaders. These strategoi (plural) commanded thousands of soldiers and were the ultimate military authorities. The word strategos comes from the Greek words *stratia* (army) and *agos* (to lead). For centuries, the existence and protection of the Greek empire relied heavily on their strategic brilliance.

While community college strategy may not be a life or death proposition, our work is profound. It changes lives. It drives economic growth and will affect current *and* future generations. As a strategic leader, many of your colleagues will look to you for guidance. They will follow your lead and their support will be an essential part of your success.

Considering all of those things: How will you lead your army?

Chapter 6

*Community College Leaders
In Their Own Words*

*I*n March of 2009, I was invited to speak at the Saguaro Correctional Center in Eloy, Arizona, a short two-hour drive from my home. The state of Hawaii sends thousands of prisoners to facilities on the mainland, citing cost as their primary reason. This particular prison houses almost 2,000 inmates, all from Hawaii. Representatives from the facility asked me to speak at a graduation ceremony for a group of inmates who recently completed either education programs or substance abuse rehabilitation programs while incarcerated.

I had planned to talk about the benefits of higher education and how continuing their education when they leave prison might open doors they assumed would otherwise be closed to them. I started my speech as planned by talking about my upbringing and the life I was able to lead largely because my parents attended college. My speech never progressed past this point.

As I looked out over the audience I realized many of the inmates had difficult childhoods that led to even more challenging adulthoods. Many of the inmates wanted a better life and seemed to be committed to taking their lives in a different direction once given the opportunity. At that moment, I decided my parents would be the focus of my speech.

Both of my parents grew up in abject poverty. My mother lost both her parents by the time she was fifteen and was forced to live on her own. My father's father died when he was three years old, leaving my grandmother to raise six children on her own. Due to the influence of teachers and mentors, my parents learned that the college path would allow them to break the poverty cycle. My parents have recently retired after successful careers in public service. My mom served as a member of Governor Ben Cayetano's cabinet from 1994-2002. My dad retired after a decades-long career running the court system in Hawaii, and finally serving as CEO of the Office of Hawaiian Affairs, a pseudo-government organization in Hawaii.

> We love our jobs as higher education leaders because our work is profound. We improve lives. We change families. We better our communities, and we impact future generations.

Their successes are impressive by any standard, but more so when one considers where they came from and the challenges they overcame. My parents were able to send my brother and I to Punahou School, the best secondary school in Hawaii (and one of the best schools in the nation—with alumni Steve Case, Barack Obama, and Pierre Omidyar). Higher education has the ability to impact generations, and I am proof of that.

After my speech, I was able to socialize with the inmates and was gratified by their positive feedback. It seemed as though my message hit home and many wrote me letters of thanks in the weeks following my visit to the prison. This past year, my three young sons were all able to attend my Ph.D. graduation ceremony at the University of Arizona and my hope is that my accomplishments in higher education will have an impact on them just as my parents' accomplishments impacted me.

This is why we do what we do. This is why our jobs are so gratifying and fulfilling. We love our jobs as higher education leaders because our work is profound. We improve lives. We change families. We better our communities, and we impact future generations.

In this chapter you will hear directly from community college leaders themselves. You will hear from the generous participants in my study across three community colleges. You will hear from presidents, vice-presidents, deans, department chairs, directors, and faculty leaders. These leaders will offer valuable insight into managing fiscal crises, achieving strategic success, and facilitating innovation. I will attempt to provide context and refer back to the prominent concepts presented in previous chapters, but I'll do my best to let their observations and analyses speak for themselves.

In Their Own Words: Strategy

There is certainly something to be said about clear, concise, transparent leadership. The President of BBCC espouses the importance of **clearly communicating institutional priorities,** and perhaps more importantly, demonstrating the administration's commitment to those priorities through the allocation of resources.

"In the last four years we've focused around several strategic priorities. Initially we were looking at three competitive advantages and how to leverage things that make us unique and things we can do better than anyone else. Priority one, two, and three—these had to be our strong driving forces. Pieces are plucked from the strategic plan that ran through 2014, but that isn't my style of planning. The plan had everything in it, and if you're trying to do everything that's not really strategic. We will start a new annual process with two or three strategic priorities and follow those. Everything new, or everything we've done in our budget process, had to be linked to one of those {priorities}. As overriding budget principles we had three things: it had to be student-centered, future-focused, and employee-friendly. Those are our guiding principles, but they must be tied to our strategic priorities."

—President, BBCC

Here is a direct quote on the same topic from the Chief Financial Officer at BBCC:

"While we haven't done well in terms of a strategic plan, we have strategic concepts that have been well-communicated— things like student-centered, future-focused, and employee-friendly. We do very well following those of high level concepts. . . We want to fund courses in our competitive advantage areas, then in concentric circles go out and see what else we can fund."

—Chief Financial Officer, CBCC

One of the items I presented in Chapter Five involved the importance of **strategic flexibility**. Here, the chief financial officer of BBCC offers his insight.

"That's where you have to be flexible as an organization to make sure you're compliant when these things happen (statutory changes and federal regulations). You can't get into a blame game and say, we had our lobbyist out there and why didn't we see this coming, but nobody did? (state allocation reductions). You just have to be able to adapt. There are big things like that and little things as well. A university is less likely to be adaptable, so being a small college with a solid administration that can sense the direction rapidly and move is important."

—Chief Financial Officer, BBCC

In Chapter Five, I defined **strategic positioning** as "the collective effort of stakeholders to shape and define the priorities, objectives, and direction of a particular institution." My research has shown that community colleges faced the fiscal crisis of state divestment with admirable intensity and passion.

This passion led them to grow even closer to their historical identities as open-access institutions that serve traditionally disadvantaged populations. The president of BBCC offers his insight.

"You can't replace the type of resources that have been lost from the state side, so you look at public private partnerships. There are opportunities, but public-private partnerships come with strings attached, and if we come to rely too heavily on those funding streams then we could fundamentally change the mission of the college."

—President, BBCC

A department chair at BBCC sees things differently.

"To me, the direction we're going is already changing and has changed our core values. I feel the direction we're going, that the college is going (and I know we're mandated to do it) but it's going away from our mission statement, which provides lifelong learning. I've been told I don't know how many times, "You've got to just concentrate on people who are seeking a degree. We don't care about the guy who wants to come in and take a welding class." That kind of thinking bothers me."

—Department Chair, BBCC

The leaders in my study embody the philosophy of **Embedded Community Colleges**. Time and time again, they cite the importance of serving their communities by forming sustainable symbiotic relationships with community stakeholders.

"I do everything I can do to be a good neighbor and I think people know that, so we are entrusted with providing educational services and community support. We do that very well, so I don't think we get the pounding on the table that some people do."

—President, GRCC

"We have a good relationship with the community and we see partnerships as key to us existing in this community. We have a lot of advisory committees for some of our degree seeking programs. They play a role as advisory committee members and tell us what classes we should teach and what skills they need. Another partnership is with the local industry association. Our president is a board member on that and they get a lot of feedback and do a lot of job training. I serve on the board of the local hospital and they fund a lot of our nursing education and our nurses of course go and work for them, so that's another big one."

—Chief Financial Officer, GRCC

"One of our missions is to serve the people in Grants and Reserves county through partnerships . . . and I'm paraphrasing, but the partnerships have always been part of our DNA. Certainly grants are a good way, in a time of cutbacks, to find funding for programs that are key and important."

—Director of Institutional Research, GRCC

The Vice President of Instruction at BBCC shared the details of an innovative partnership with private industry.

". . . with co-op, internships, and those kinds of things, business and industry play a big part. In some cases they can be the key for in-kind financial resources. I would say that can be institutionally specific, based on how the institution operates and where. The best place I've ever been for that aspect was up in (another state), because we had a relationship with John Deere. We had a credit based diesel program tied into John Deere. At any point in time they might drop off a half a dozen combines, tractors and other equipment. We were probably using several million dollars of stuff we didn't pay a nickel for, which is a hell of a big deal."

—Vice President of Instruction, BBCC

In Chapter Four, I introduced the concept of the **Quartering of Community Colleges** as a framework to organize and explain the different pressures that exert influence on community colleges. This goes along with the concept of a **Mandate to Neutralize,** which helps explain the strategic importance of activities designed to *manage* the quartering pulls of those external pressures. The next section contains a few quotes from community college leaders who offer details about implementing both concepts.

"We are sitting at a point of balance and trying to stay there. We're experiencing interesting pressure from various constituencies that affect our ability to stay in balance, as you might imagine...We're beholden to a lot of stakeholders. Of course there's always our taxpayers who give us some of our funding, and we try to be as sensitive as we can to their needs, especially because we recognize this area is not as affluent as other places. And there's the state legislature, which has some decision-making authority and regulatory authority over us."

—Director of Institutional Research, CBCC

"We comply to the federal government. We comply to (accrediting body). We comply to the state. We're doing constant reporting. Constant procedure changes. The Clery Act; the new regs on sexual assault. We're able to keep up now, but I imagine when the new higher education act is reauthorized, which should be shortly, we'll have to do another data hire, or something like that. They're taking comments now. It's huge and, as I told the legislature, I've said it specifically to house appropriations: "I can either educate students or I can comply. Which do you want because it's getting to the point where we can't do both."

—President, CBCC

"Most of our students attend part-time and they take almost four years on average to complete. Many of the metrics are looking at the three year completion rate, and those are blunt instruments that don't connect well with our mission, or with our specific community needs. So my job is to come up with strategies that can deal with those separate sectors (state and federal regulators) and try to combine the resources in a way that won't shoot ourselves in the foot. It's a bit of a juggling act, and that's one of the pressures."

—Director of Institutional Research, GRCC

"Donors and possible donors can definitely influence an institution if you let them. A military installation commander can extremely influence us. The federal government changes in financial aid is an influence. What has that done to our enrollment? What are the financial impacts of that? Huge. All sorts of externalities can kill you."

—Chief Financial Officer, BBCC

In Chapter Five, I shared the example of CBCC's extraordinary **strategic foresight** in understanding the community college ecosystem and the pressures exerting influence on them. Here are two direct quotes from the Chief Financial Officer of CBCC regarding that approach.

"We made some tough decisions, but we started early. And because we started early, anticipating there would be cuts to our state aid, in particular our operating state aid, we've been able to respond in a much more strategic and planned way and not had knee jerk reactions to the situation."

—Chief Financial Officer, CBCC

"We started making adjustments at least two years before the actual cut, so when the cut occurred, two things happened. One, we were expecting it. Two, because (specific type of additional aid CBCC receives) was not affected, the cut wasn't nearly as damaging to us as it could've been. We had made conscientious efforts legislatively and with the governor's office as CBCC to try and preserve (specific type of additional aid CBCC receives)."

—Chief Financial Officer, CBCC

In Chapter Five, I highlighted the efforts of CBCC's president to aggressively implement **shared governance procedures** at CBCC. A positive byproduct of shared governance was that when the administration chose to make unpopular decisions, they had already involved faculty and staff members. Therefore, those difficult decisions were graciously accepted, as opposed to vigorously protested. Here we have a direct quote for CBCC's Vice President of Instructor and Director of Institutional Research.

"Important faculty and staff committees have been put together and given duties. That's always a learning process when you first start doing it, and I gathered the leadership prior to (current president) was more corporate in its culture, more directive. She has really opened up a lot more shared processes, so we're having to learn how to live that way."

—Director of Institutional Research, CBCC

"It (strategic planning) helps you establish core values, so the president preaches and buys into shared governance. We don't just pay lip service to it. We do it and it's harder and slower, but in the long run you get a better outcome because you have some buy-in."

- Vice President of Instruction, CBCC

The President of GRCC offered this comment on the **resilience of community colleges**.

"Community colleges, I believe, have been their worst enemies over the years, because no matter what the funding structure was, community colleges always met the need one way or another. That says to the legislature and the governor, we can continue cutting, no problem, because they're making it work."

—President, GRCC

In Chapters Four and Five, I discussed the phenomenon of the **isomorphic huddle**; community college leaders increasing their collaborative activities through statewide associations designed to manage the fiscal crisis and neutralize future impacts on community colleges. The presidents of all community colleges in this state decided to create a clearinghouse that would represent the interests of all the colleges in the state.

"Now the key thing, moving forward, is creating the (statewide group). It will be a voluntary association creating a one stop shop for all community college issues. We don't have a one go-to place for all things community college, so you either get one college having to speak for everyone, or even worse, you get someone who doesn't know about community colleges speaking for us. This organization will allow for a one stop place, but still leave community colleges their sovereignty, their own decisions. But we will coordinate together."

—President, BBCC

The Chief Financial Officer of BBCC also commented on this phenomenon.

"... when everyone feels pressured, you tend to group together and I think that helped us solidify ourselves. We (CFO statewide group) are a far more candid group than the presidents will ever be. The presidents play poker. We discuss strategies. So some of the things we've discussed, particularly when our budgets were being hacked by the state, is what statutory things we should not have to do, since the state is defunding us. We had those discussions.

—Chief Financial Officer, BBCC

In Their Own Words: Finances

Leaders in my study faced what will probably be the greatest challenge of their careers. State government had just cut allocations to community colleges by 50 percent. This drastic cut meant the collective identities of these institutions would be tested as leaders scrambled to neutralize the damage, while struggling to serve hordes of students who flocked to them because of the downturn in the economy. The strategies they implemented were complex, remarkable, and made my research a story of triumph rather than tragedy.

This section contains direct quotes from many of the leaders cited in the section above. All quotes relate specifically to the great state divestment in higher education, fiscal crises, and efforts to manage those pressures.

As presented in Chapter Five, community college leaders aggressively stashed money in **reserve accounts** to help fill the gap of lost state allocations and protect themselves against future cuts. Many also implemented **aggressive cost-cutting/ efficiency initiatives**.

"In general BBCC is still financially solvent. It's in a good financial position largely because about ten years ago senior administration. which didn't include me, made some very good strategic moves regarding financial capturability and setting aside governing board reserves for future investments. When I came here in 2007 there was a significant reserve base."

—Chief Financial Officer, BBCC

"I can say that in each of the last six years we've had good years. We've increased our unrestricted fund balance each year and been able to operate within our means, meaning that from a financial situation, whatever budget we set, we were able to actually do. In just about every case, we were able to reduce our expenditures throughout the year so we didn't spend the entire budget. From an expense side, as well as the revenue side, we tried to look at different opportunities"

—President, GRCC

"We have a longstanding practice of maintaining a reasonable cash reserve, which has been highly supported by our board, and is apparently somewhat unusual. We get a lot of flak from certain community members for having, what do they call it? Excess cash on hand. Whereas, in our minds, if state funding goes away, which it very well could, we'd like to have at least six months' operating costs so we can get our students out in good shape. We have a contingency plan, because we've been told in no uncertain terms by certain legislators that funding will go away at some point."

—Director of Institutional Research, CBCC

In Chapter Three, I quoted a community college president outside my study who asked me rhetorically "At what point can we stop answering the phone (when state government calls)?" The president of BBCC shared strong words with me along those same lines.

"If the state wants to play a prominent role, then they need to step-up and fund. That's easy for me to say because still a huge portion of my overall budget comes from state aid, but if I was (other, less dependent community colleges), I wonder at times if they don't say, "Take the remaining million dollars and leave us alone." I don't have that luxury. I'm still highly dependent on the state for funding."

—President, BBCC

The president of BBCC opened up about the **severity of the fiscal crisis** and the approach he and his administration were taking in response to state allocation reductions.

"Over the last four years we've probably lost 25 to 35 percent of our state aid . . . Clearly we have county taxes that come in. I will say that the financially stability of the college is still there, so some reserves were built up, but we've had to make significant adjustments. We've had to make reductions in force. We deleted certain things, but we have not had to panic. We've got all the low hanging fruit. We've cut most of the fat, and we're now down to where the shrinking resources have become significant. I'm not necessarily concerned about fiscal year 2014, but I'm very concerned about fiscal year 2015, unless things change radically . . . We are not in crisis mode, but we are to the point where things are tight."

—President, BBCC

The president of CBCC offered her institution's response to the **drastic state reductions.**

"The first step was one I needed to take, which was basically RIF (reduction in force) in the administration, bringing us into what I thought was a more realistic administration for the budget structure we were gonna be facing. We went from three vice presidents to two. We went from six deans to three, and from five divisions to three. I also consolidated a lot of divisions, and of course the administrative staff associated with those positions. We probably right off the bat cut close to a million dollars from our budget."

—President, CBCC

Afterword

*A*s I enter my tenth year as a community college leader, I understand that in many ways my journey has just begun. My research has certainly given me a deeper understanding as to what it means to be a strategically successful community college leader.

My journey has, and will, continue to take me to different community colleges across the nation and I am always struck by the passion of today's community college leaders. We are truly an inspirational group of professionals. We understand the importance of our jobs and we strive to find innovative ways to be successful despite tremendous challenges. My experience working at community colleges has ignited a passion that will no doubt last my entire professional career.

I hope this book has provided you with the tools to be a successful community college leader and given you some strategic perspective. As a leader, I encourage you to never stop searching for ways to create strategic success and to exude innovation. As you proceed on *your* journey, I wish you all the best.

I leave you with an ancient Hawaiian proverb: E kuhikuhi pono i na au iki a me na au nui o ka `ike. "Instruct well in both the little and the great currents of knowledge"

Appendix—Workbooks

Chapter 4: The Community College Ecosystem—Workbook

Quartering Concept:
Consider each category of pressures in the quartering diagram below:

The Quartering of Community Colleges

Community
- Industry groups
- Advisory boards
- Local governing boards
- Military partners

State Gov't
- Legislators
- Governors
- Political groups

The Community College

Regulators
- Accreditors
- Universities
- State statutes
- Federal regulations/laws

Other CCs
- Sister schools
- National CC trends
- Higher ed trends (STEM)

Circle or highlight the three most influential pressures in your role as a community college leader. (see next page)

Mandate to Neutralize:

Considering the strategies introduced in the *Mandate to Neutralize* section (page 84), identify how you might manage or neutralize these specific quartering pressures.

Pressure #1 (**):**

_____

_____

_____

_____

Pressure #2 (**):**

_____

_____

_____

_____

Pressure #3 (**):**

_____

_____

_____

_____

Discussion Questions:

Are you involved in any isomorphic huddling activities?

Yes   No

If so, how have these activities benefited your community college?

_____

_____

_____

Considering the current identity of community colleges and the community college ecosystem, how might the strategic position of community colleges be different far into the future?

_____

_____

_____

_____

_____

_____

_____

_____

_____

_____

_____

_____

_____

_____

_____

_____

_____

_____

_____

_____

_____

Chapter 5: Community College Strategy—Workbook

Select two of the nine examples presented in Chapter 5 that you believe would have a significant impact on your institution. Present a detailed plan for strategic success related to those two examples.

Example #1 (_____ **):**

_____

_____

_____

_____

_____

_____

_____

Example #2 (_____ **):**

_____

_____

_____

_____

_____

_____

_____

_____

_____

_____

_____

Chapter 6: Community College Leaders—Workbook

Your task in this section will be to interview two respected, innovative leaders at your institution. Your interview will consist of the following four questions taken directly from my interviews with other community college leaders:

Please describe the strategic strengths of your institution.

_____

_____

_____

_____

_____

_____

What are the main challenges associated with reduced financial resources (decreased state allocations for example)?

_____

_____

_____

_____

_____

Which entities exert the most pressure on you in your role as a community college leader?

_____

_____

_____

_____

What strategies do you employ to manage those pressures?

_____

_____

_____

_____

_____

_____

_____

_____

_____

_____

_____

_____

_____

_____

_____

_____

_____

_____

_____

Acknowledgements

I often say this book is an extension of my dissertation research, which it is. But that may be an oversimplification, because this book is based *largely* on my dissertation research. Considering that, I need to acknowledge the many community college leaders who contributed to my research as interviewees. Although I cannot list you by name, you know who you are. Please know that this book could not exist without you and your willingness to generously share your valuable time with me at Bridge and Buffer Community College, Grants and Reserves Community College, and Crystal Ball Community College. I am a fan of all of you and will forever be a fan of each of your institutions. Thank you.

I want to acknowledge Dr. Regina Deil-Amen, Dr. Ozan Jaquette, and Dr. Gary Rhoades for shaping my research and analysis. They pushed me to the highest levels of contemplation and by challenging me, made my research meaningful. As respected scholars and authors, I could not have asked for better mentors. Thank you for pushing me as hard as you did.

I want to thank my editor and publisher Sammie Justesen and NorLightsPress for making this dream a reality. I am so very proud of what we created. Thank you for believing in me and for believing in this book.

I can easily attribute my drive and ambition to the hardest working people I know: my parents. They achieved enormous success despite every possible obstacle. They are my inspiration. They worked hard to give me every advantage growing up and

I owe much of my success to them. Thanks mom and dad. This book is yours as well.

To my sons Kekoa, Maika, and Kainoa: You are my motivation to not only be successful, but to be a father you can be proud of. Never stop wanting to play with your dad, Dada.

A special thanks goes to Dr. John Morton who oversees the entire community college system in Hawaii. He is an impressive community college leader by any metric, having served in all levels of leadership throughout his career. Thank you for taking time out of your impossibly busy schedule to write such an eloquent and inspiring foreword to this book.

About the Author

Dr. Clyne G. H. Namuo earned a Ph.D. in Higher Education Strategy from the University of Arizona's Center for the Study of Higher Education where his published dissertation research involved the impact of reduced financial resources on the strategic positioning of community colleges. He has held a variety of positions in the field of information technology in Honolulu, HI and San Diego, CA. He has taught in the University of  Hawaii Community College System, San Diego Community College District, and is currently the Department Chair for computer information systems at Cochise College in Arizona. He lives in Sierra Vista, Arizona with his wife Tiana, his three sons, and two step-daughters. Find more information at http://www.communitycollegestrategy.com .

CPSIA information can be obtained
at www.ICGtesting.com
Printed in the USA
FSOW02n1345250215
5330FS

9 781935 254966